Payments for Ecosystem Services: Scaling Nature-Based Solutions for Sustainable Development and Climate Resilience

I0029950

Copyright

Table of Contents

Preface

As the world faces escalating environmental challenges, the urgency of finding sustainable solutions has never been greater. Climate change, biodiversity loss, and water scarcity are no longer distant threats but pressing realities that demand immediate and transformative action. Amidst these challenges, nature itself offers the most effective solutions. By leveraging ecosystem services, we can mitigate climate risks, enhance resilience, and restore the delicate balance between human activity and the natural world.

This book explores the pivotal role of Payments for Ecosystem Services (PES) in scaling Nature-Based Solutions (NBS) for sustainable development and climate resilience. PES provides a mechanism to value and incentivize the conservation and restoration of ecosystems, ensuring that those who maintain nature's services are fairly compensated. From carbon sequestration to watershed protection, PES has the potential to bridge the financing gap for NBS, unlocking long-term environmental and socio-economic benefits.

However, despite its promise, PES is not a one-size-fits-all solution. Its success depends on well-designed frameworks, effective governance, and equitable benefit-sharing. Through this book, we delve into the theory, policy, and practice of PES, outlining how it can be optimized to support NBS across different landscapes and sectors.

The need for bold, scalable, and financially sustainable climate solutions has never been more critical. PES offers a pathway to incentivize sustainable land and water management, ensuring that investments in nature yield dividends for both present and future generations. By harnessing the power of markets, policies, and community engagement, PES can transform environmental conservation from an unfunded ideal into a viable economic strategy.

This book aims to equip policymakers, practitioners, researchers, and investors with the knowledge to implement PES effectively, driving the transition toward a nature-positive future. The path ahead requires collaboration, innovation, and a commitment to aligning economic incentives with ecological integrity. With the right strategies in place, PES can play a transformative role in shaping a resilient and sustainable world.

Introduction: Unlocking the Potential of PES for Scaling NBS

NBS have emerged as essential tools for addressing some of the most pressing environmental challenges of our time, from mitigating climate change to enhancing biodiversity and supporting sustainable development. These solutions, rooted in the protection, restoration, and sustainable management of ecosystems, offer a way to address complex global issues while providing co-benefits for communities, economies, and the environment.

However, the implementation and scaling of NBS often face significant financial and institutional barriers. PES schemes provide a promising mechanism to overcome these challenges. By placing a tangible value on the benefits ecosystems deliver—such as clean water, carbon sequestration, and flood control—PES schemes create incentives for stakeholders to invest in and sustain NBS initiatives.

This chapter explores the interplay between PES and NBS, examining how PES schemes can mobilize the resources needed to implement and expand NBS projects. It sets the stage for the broader discussion in the book, providing an overview of NBS, the principles of PES, and the synergistic potential of these two approaches to drive environmental and social resilience. In doing so, it highlights the critical role of PES in bridging the financing gap for NBS, offering a pathway to a more sustainable future.

Overview of NBS and Their Importance

NBS are approaches that use natural processes and ecosystem services to address societal challenges. They are designed to protect, manage, and restore ecosystems to deliver benefits for both human well-being and biodiversity. As a flexible and sustainable approach, NBS integrates ecological, economic, and social considerations, making it a vital tool for tackling issues such as climate change, biodiversity loss, and resource scarcity.

At the core of NBS is the recognition that healthy ecosystems provide critical services essential for life on Earth. Forests act as carbon sinks, reducing greenhouse gas concentrations, while wetlands improve water quality and regulate floodwaters. Coastal ecosystems such as mangroves buffer storm surges, protecting vulnerable communities. These services not only mitigate environmental risks but also support livelihoods, enhance public health, and contribute to economic resilience.

NBS aligns closely with global sustainability goals, including the United Nations Sustainable Development Goals (SDGs). For example, reforestation projects contribute to SDG 13 on climate action by sequestering carbon, while sustainable urban planning integrates green spaces to meet SDG 11 on sustainable cities and communities. By addressing interconnected challenges, NBS offers a holistic approach to development that benefits both people and the planet.

One of the significant advantages of NBS is its adaptability. Whether implemented in urban, rural, or coastal areas, these solutions can be tailored to local contexts and integrated into existing systems. Urban areas, for instance, can benefit from green roofs and parks that reduce heat, improve air quality, and foster biodiversity. In agricultural regions, practices such as agroforestry enhance soil health and increase resilience to drought.

Despite their potential, NBS remain underutilized due to financial, institutional, and technical barriers. Scaling up NBS requires coordinated efforts to mobilize resources, foster cross-sector collaboration, and ensure long-term sustainability. This is where PES schemes play a crucial role by incentivizing investments in NBS and creating mechanisms for sustainable financing.

In summary, NBS represent an innovative and essential approach to addressing global environmental challenges. By harnessing the power of nature, they provide cost-effective, adaptable, and multifunctional solutions that align with the urgent need for sustainable development and climate resilience.

Introduction to PES: Key Concepts and Evolution

PES is a market-based mechanism designed to incentivize the conservation and sustainable management of ecosystems by compensating individuals or communities who maintain or enhance ecosystem services. These services include vital benefits that nature provides, such as clean water, carbon storage, biodiversity conservation, and flood mitigation. By assigning a monetary value to these services, PES schemes create a framework for their recognition and protection.

The core principles of PES include voluntary participation, conditionality, and additionality. Voluntary participation ensures that agreements between service providers and beneficiaries are mutually agreed upon rather than imposed. Conditionality means that payments are made only if the agreed-upon ecosystem services are delivered or maintained. Additionality ensures that the activities supported by PES schemes provide benefits that would not have occurred otherwise, making them an effective tool for addressing environmental degradation.

The evolution of PES can be traced back to the late 20th century when the concept gained traction as part of broader discussions on sustainable development and environmental economics. Early PES initiatives often focused on watershed protection, where downstream users such as municipalities or industries compensated upstream landholders for maintaining forest cover to ensure clean and reliable water flows. Over time, PES schemes expanded to address a wider range of ecosystem services, including biodiversity conservation, carbon sequestration, and landscape restoration.

The development of PES has been shaped by the increasing recognition of the economic value of ecosystem services. Studies such as the Millennium Ecosystem Assessment (2005) and The

Economics of Ecosystems and Biodiversity (TEEB) report have highlighted the critical role ecosystems play in supporting human well-being and the high costs of their degradation. These findings have underscored the need for innovative financing mechanisms like PES to bridge the gap between ecological conservation and economic development.

PES schemes can take various forms depending on their structure and objectives. Public PES programs are often government-led and funded through environmental taxes or public budgets, targeting large-scale initiatives such as reforestation or wetland restoration. Private PES schemes involve agreements between businesses and landowners, such as companies paying farmers to adopt practices that reduce carbon emissions. Hybrid schemes combine public and private funding, leveraging resources from multiple stakeholders.

While PES has shown great promise, its implementation is not without challenges. Issues such as equitable benefit distribution, land tenure security, and ensuring compliance with conditionality need to be carefully addressed. Additionally, the success of PES schemes often depends on robust governance frameworks, clear legal mechanisms, and the active participation of all stakeholders.

PES represents a transformative approach to valuing and conserving ecosystem services. By linking ecological stewardship with economic incentives, PES has evolved into a critical tool for promoting sustainable development and addressing environmental challenges, particularly in the context of NBS.

The Synergy Between PES and NBS: How PES Schemes Support Financing and Scaling

NBS and PES are complementary approaches that, when integrated, offer a powerful mechanism for addressing environmental and social challenges. NBS focus on harnessing natural processes to provide sustainable solutions to issues like climate change, biodiversity loss, and water scarcity. PES, as a financing tool, ensures the economic viability of these solutions by directly linking ecosystem service providers with beneficiaries who are willing to pay for the benefits derived. This synergy makes PES a vital enabler for implementing and scaling NBS projects.

The financial sustainability of NBS often depends on creating mechanisms that align ecological benefits with economic incentives. PES schemes achieve this by valuing the ecosystem services provided by NBS, such as carbon sequestration, flood mitigation, water purification, and biodiversity conservation. For instance, a PES scheme might pay a community to restore wetlands, recognizing the critical role wetlands play in regulating water flows and improving water quality. This financial support incentivizes local stakeholders to actively participate in and sustain NBS initiatives.

PES schemes also address a key barrier to scaling NBS: the lack of upfront funding for project implementation. Many NBS projects, such as large-scale reforestation or coastal restoration, require significant initial investments. PES provides a structured framework for mobilizing these resources, drawing on public funding, private sector contributions, or a combination of both. Carbon markets, biodiversity offsets, and green taxes can be integrated into PES schemes to channel funds toward NBS projects, creating a steady revenue stream that ensures long-term viability.

Another strength of PES in supporting NBS is its capacity to foster stakeholder collaboration. NBS projects often require the involvement of multiple actors, including landowners, businesses, governments, and communities. PES serves as a unifying mechanism by creating transparent agreements where service providers are compensated for actions that benefit others. For example, farmers practicing agroforestry can receive payments from downstream water users who benefit from improved water quality and reduced erosion. This shared responsibility fosters trust and cooperation, which are essential for the success of NBS initiatives.

The scalability of PES schemes also makes them particularly effective for NBS. By structuring payments based on measurable outcomes, PES creates a replicable model that can be applied across different regions and ecosystems. For instance, a PES scheme designed to enhance biodiversity in one region can be adapted to protect marine ecosystems in another, leveraging lessons learned to improve effectiveness. This adaptability is crucial for scaling NBS to address global environmental challenges.

Furthermore, PES ensures that the benefits of NBS are distributed equitably among stakeholders. By providing financial incentives, PES schemes enable marginalized communities and small-scale landowners to participate in NBS projects, empowering them to become active stewards of the environment. This inclusivity enhances the social and economic impact of NBS while ensuring that conservation efforts do not come at the expense of vulnerable groups.

Despite its potential, the integration of PES and NBS requires careful design and implementation to address challenges such as ensuring additionality, avoiding unintended consequences, and maintaining the integrity of ecosystem services over time. Robust governance frameworks, clear monitoring mechanisms, and stakeholder engagement are essential to maximizing the synergy between these approaches.

Overall, PES and NBS are inherently aligned in their objectives, with PES providing the financial and structural support needed to implement and scale NBS effectively. By bridging the gap between ecological conservation and economic development, PES schemes ensure the long-term viability of NBS, helping to create resilient ecosystems and sustainable communities. This synergy represents a transformative approach to tackling global environmental challenges in a way that benefits both people and nature.

Objectives and Structure of the Book

The goal of this book is to explore the potential of PES schemes as a critical financial mechanism for implementing and scaling NBS. It aims to provide a comprehensive understanding of how PES can bridge the gap between ecological conservation and economic incentives, creating a pathway for sustainable development. By examining the theoretical foundations, practical frameworks, and future directions of PES, the book seeks to equip policymakers, practitioners, researchers, and stakeholders with the knowledge needed to design, implement, and scale PES schemes effectively in support of NBS.

The book's primary objectives are as follows:

1. **Introduce PES and its relevance to NBS**: Establish the principles and components of PES while demonstrating its alignment with the objectives of NBS.

2. **Provide practical guidance on PES design and implementation**: Explore how PES schemes can be structured to finance NBS projects, addressing challenges and leveraging opportunities.

3. **Examine governance and institutional frameworks**: Highlight the importance of legal, policy, and institutional arrangements in ensuring the success of PES schemes.

4. **Explore financing mechanisms for scaling NBS**: Analyze how public, private, and blended funding can be mobilized through PES to support large-scale NBS initiatives.

5. **Address monitoring and evaluation needs**: Discuss tools and techniques for ensuring the effectiveness and sustainability of PES-supported NBS projects.

6. **Highlight social and ethical dimensions**: Emphasize the importance of equity, inclusivity, and ethical considerations in the design and implementation of PES schemes.

7. **Provide a forward-looking perspective**: Outline emerging trends, innovative applications, and policy recommendations for integrating PES and NBS at scale.

The structure of the book is organized to systematically build knowledge and insights, beginning with foundational concepts and advancing toward practical applications and future opportunities:

1. **Introduction**: Lays the groundwork by explaining the importance of NBS, the principles of PES, and the synergy between the two.

2. **Theoretical Foundations**: Provides a deep dive into the ecosystem services framework, PES principles, and their alignment with NBS.

3. **Designing PES Schemes**: Focuses on structuring PES schemes to effectively support NBS projects, including practical considerations and common challenges.

4. **Governance and Institutions**: Discusses the role of legal, regulatory, and institutional frameworks in enabling successful PES schemes.

5. **Financing Mechanisms**: Explores diverse funding sources and financial tools for scaling NBS through PES.

6. **Monitoring and Evaluation**: Highlights the importance of assessing PES schemes to ensure their effectiveness and sustainability.

7. **Scaling Up PES**: Examines strategies for expanding PES-supported NBS initiatives, emphasizing partnerships and innovation.

8. **Social and Ethical Dimensions**: Analyzes the equity, inclusivity, and ethical considerations necessary for ensuring the success and fairness of PES schemes.

9. **Future Directions**: Concludes with emerging trends, innovative approaches, and policy recommendations for the integration of PES and NBS.

By structuring the book in this way, readers will gain a step-by-step understanding of how PES schemes can be harnessed to finance and scale NBS, creating solutions that benefit both ecosystems and societies. The book ultimately seeks to inspire and inform efforts to address global environmental challenges through innovative and sustainable approaches.

Chapter 1: Theoretical Foundations of PES and NBS

This chapter explores the foundational concepts underlying PES and NBS, focusing on their shared reliance on ecosystem services. It examines the categories of ecosystem services and their critical role, the key principles of PES such as conditionality and additionality, and the diverse applications of NBS. The chapter also highlights how these approaches align with global sustainability goals, providing a theoretical basis for understanding how PES can support and scale NBS.

Understanding Ecosystem Services and Their Categories

Ecosystem services are the benefits that humans derive from natural ecosystems. These services are critical to sustaining life on Earth, supporting economic activities, and enhancing human well-being. They are broadly categorized into four types: provisioning, regulating, cultural, and supporting services. Understanding these categories helps to clarify the value ecosystems provide and their role in addressing environmental and societal challenges.

Provisioning Services

Provisioning services are the tangible goods that ecosystems provide. These include food, fresh water, raw materials, and medicinal resources. For example, agricultural crops, fisheries, and forestry products are essential for human survival and economic development. Freshwater ecosystems supply clean water for drinking, irrigation, and industrial use, while biodiversity provides genetic resources that support crop breeding and pharmaceutical development. The availability and quality of provisioning services are directly influenced by the health and functionality of ecosystems.

Regulating Services

Regulating services involve the natural processes that ecosystems perform to maintain environmental stability. These include climate regulation, water purification, flood control, and pest management. Forests, for instance, act as carbon sinks, reducing greenhouse gases and mitigating climate change. Wetlands filter pollutants and regulate water flows, reducing the risk of flooding and ensuring water quality. Pollination, provided by bees and other insects, is another critical regulating service that supports food production. By buffering environmental changes and reducing risks, regulating services enhance resilience and sustainability.

Cultural Services

Cultural services are the non-material benefits that ecosystems provide to humans. These include recreational, aesthetic, educational, and spiritual experiences. Natural landscapes, such as mountains, forests, and beaches, contribute to human well-being by offering spaces for leisure, tourism, and inspiration. Cultural services also include the traditional knowledge and practices tied to ecosystems, which shape local identities and heritage. While these services are less tangible, their value is evident in their contribution to mental health, cultural preservation, and economic opportunities such as eco-tourism.

Supporting Services

Supporting services are the foundational processes that underpin the functioning of ecosystems and the delivery of other ecosystem services. These include nutrient cycling, soil formation, photosynthesis, and habitat provision. For example, nutrient cycling ensures the availability of essential elements for plant growth, while photosynthesis drives energy flow in ecosystems. Supporting services are often indirect and long-term, but they are critical for maintaining the overall health and productivity of ecosystems.

Summary

Ecosystem services provide essential benefits that sustain life, economies, and cultures. Recognizing these services in their distinct categories—provisioning, regulating, cultural, and supporting—highlights the diverse and interconnected ways in which ecosystems contribute to human well-being. This understanding is crucial for designing mechanisms, such as PES, to incentivize their conservation and sustainable management. By valuing and protecting ecosystem services, societies can ensure that these benefits continue to flow for current and future generations.

Principles of PES: Voluntary Transactions, Conditionality, Additionality, and Stakeholder Participation

PES schemes are designed to incentivize the conservation and sustainable management of ecosystems by providing financial or in-kind rewards for maintaining or enhancing ecosystem services. The effectiveness and credibility of PES depend on adhering to core principles that guide their design and implementation. These principles include voluntary transactions, conditionality, additionality, and stakeholder participation. Together, they ensure that PES schemes are equitable, efficient, and impactful.

Voluntary Transactions

Voluntary participation is a cornerstone of PES schemes. Both service providers, such as landowners or communities, and service buyers, such as governments, businesses, or individuals, must willingly engage in the transaction. This ensures that agreements are based on mutual consent rather than coercion, fostering trust and collaboration among stakeholders. Voluntary transactions allow participants to negotiate terms that align with their interests and capacities, making PES more adaptable to diverse contexts.

For example, a farmer may agree to adopt agroforestry practices in exchange for payments from a water utility company that benefits from improved water quality. In such cases, the voluntary nature of the agreement ensures that the farmer's needs and constraints are considered, while the utility company receives a service it values. This mutual benefit strengthens the long-term sustainability of the PES arrangement.

Conditionality

Conditionality is a defining feature of PES schemes, requiring that payments be tied to the delivery or maintenance of specific ecosystem services. This principle ensures that payments are not made upfront or unconditionally but are instead contingent upon measurable outcomes. Conditionality provides accountability and guarantees that financial resources are effectively used to achieve environmental objectives.

For instance, a PES scheme targeting reforestation may stipulate that payments are made only after a certain number of trees have been planted and monitored for survival over a set period. Similarly, a wetland restoration project might require regular water quality testing to verify the achievement of agreed-upon goals. Conditionality thus creates a clear link between payments and performance, incentivizing participants to fulfill their commitments.

However, implementing conditionality can be challenging, as it requires robust monitoring and verification mechanisms. These systems must be transparent, cost-effective, and accessible to all stakeholders to ensure compliance without imposing excessive burdens.

Additionality

Additionality refers to the principle that PES schemes should lead to benefits that would not have occurred without the intervention. This ensures that PES payments create a net positive impact on ecosystem services rather than subsidizing activities that would have taken place anyway. Additionality is critical for the credibility and effectiveness of PES, as it prevents the misuse of funds and maximizes environmental gains.

For example, if a PES scheme pays landowners to preserve forests that were already under legal protection, the scheme fails to meet the additionality criterion. In contrast, payments that incentivize the conversion of degraded lands into forests represent true additionality, as they generate new environmental benefits.

Ensuring additionality requires careful baseline assessments to determine the existing state of ecosystem services and the likelihood of changes without the PES intervention. By establishing clear baselines, PES schemes can set realistic targets and measure their incremental impact over time.

Stakeholder Participation

Active stakeholder participation is essential for the success of PES schemes. Stakeholders, including service providers, buyers, and intermediaries, must be involved in the design, implementation, and monitoring of PES arrangements. This inclusivity ensures that diverse perspectives are considered, leading to fairer and more effective outcomes.

In many cases, service providers are small-scale landowners, indigenous communities, or marginalized groups who depend on natural resources for their livelihoods. Engaging these stakeholders in decision-making processes helps address their needs and concerns while empowering them as custodians of ecosystem services. For example, involving local communities in a PES scheme for watershed protection can foster a sense of ownership and responsibility, improving compliance and long-term success.

Participation also extends to buyers and intermediaries, who play critical roles in funding, managing, and facilitating PES schemes. Transparent communication and collaborative decision-making among all parties help build trust, resolve conflicts, and ensure equitable benefit-sharing.

However, achieving meaningful participation can be complex, particularly in contexts with power imbalances or conflicting interests. Capacity-building initiatives, such as training and awareness programs, can enhance stakeholders' ability to engage effectively and advocate for their rights.

Interplay Between Principles

The principles of voluntary transactions, conditionality, additionality, and stakeholder participation are interdependent, and their successful implementation requires careful integration. For example, conditionality and additionality depend on robust stakeholder participation to establish clear baselines, define performance metrics, and ensure compliance. Similarly, voluntary transactions are more likely to succeed when stakeholders are actively involved and trust the fairness of the process.

Balancing these principles requires adaptive management, as PES schemes often operate in dynamic and complex socio-ecological contexts. Flexibility in design and implementation can help address challenges while maintaining the integrity of these principles.

Summary

The principles of PES provide a framework for creating effective, equitable, and accountable mechanisms to conserve and enhance ecosystem services. Voluntary transactions ensure stakeholder buy-in and adaptability, conditionality guarantees that payments are tied to outcomes, additionality maximizes the impact of interventions, and stakeholder participation fosters inclusivity and trust. By adhering to these principles, PES schemes can serve as a reliable tool for financing and scaling NBS, contributing to global sustainability efforts.

NBS Typologies: Restoration, Conservation, and Sustainable Use

NBS encompass a wide range of approaches to address societal challenges while simultaneously protecting, managing, and enhancing ecosystems. These approaches are broadly categorized into three typologies: restoration, conservation, and sustainable use. Each typology plays a unique role in supporting environmental resilience, social well-being, and economic sustainability. Understanding these typologies is essential for designing and implementing effective NBS projects.

Restoration

Restoration focuses on rehabilitating degraded ecosystems to restore their functionality and biodiversity. This typology aims to reverse environmental damage caused by human activities such as deforestation, pollution, and unsustainable land use. By restoring ecosystems, restoration-based NBS enhance the delivery of ecosystem services such as carbon sequestration, water purification, and habitat provision.

Examples of restoration-based NBS include reforestation, wetland rehabilitation, and coral reef restoration. Reforestation projects, for instance, aim to re-establish forest cover on deforested or degraded lands, contributing to climate mitigation by absorbing carbon dioxide. Wetland restoration improves water quality and flood control by reintroducing native vegetation and natural hydrological processes. Similarly, restoring coral reefs enhances marine biodiversity while protecting coastal communities from storm surges.

Restoration-based NBS often require significant upfront investments and long-term commitments to ensure success. They rely on robust planning, stakeholder engagement, and adaptive management to address challenges such as invasive species, changing climate conditions, and socio-economic pressures.

Conservation

Conservation-based NBS focus on protecting intact ecosystems to maintain their ecological integrity and the services they provide. These approaches prioritize the preservation of natural areas such as forests, wetlands, grasslands, and marine ecosystems that are relatively undisturbed by human activities. Conservation efforts are critical for preventing further loss of biodiversity and mitigating the impacts of climate change.

Key conservation strategies include the establishment of protected areas, sustainable land-use planning, and ecosystem monitoring. Protected areas, such as national parks and wildlife reserves, are designed to safeguard critical habitats and species. These areas often serve as natural carbon sinks, contribute to water regulation, and provide spaces for recreation and cultural enrichment. Conservation also extends to privately-owned lands, where incentive-based mechanisms, such as PES, encourage landowners to adopt conservation practices.

While conservation is cost-effective compared to restoration, it often faces challenges related to land-use conflicts, lack of funding, and limited enforcement of regulations. Collaborative governance and community involvement are essential for overcoming these barriers and ensuring the long-term success of conservation-based NBS.

Sustainable Use

Sustainable use-based NBS focus on managing ecosystems in a way that allows for the extraction of resources while maintaining their ecological balance. This typology integrates conservation principles with socio-economic development, ensuring that resource use does not compromise the ability of ecosystems to regenerate and provide services in the future.

Examples of sustainable use-based NBS include agroforestry, sustainable fisheries, and integrated water resource management.

Agroforestry systems combine agricultural practices with tree cultivation, enhancing soil fertility, reducing erosion, and increasing carbon storage. Sustainable fisheries implement quotas and seasonal restrictions to prevent overfishing, ensuring the long-term viability of marine resources. Integrated water resource management seeks to balance water use for agriculture, industry, and communities while maintaining ecosystem health.

Sustainable use-based NBS are particularly important in regions where communities depend directly on natural resources for their livelihoods. These approaches create opportunities for income generation and poverty alleviation while promoting environmental stewardship. However, their success depends on the establishment of clear guidelines, monitoring mechanisms, and equitable benefit-sharing arrangements.

Interconnections and Synergies

While restoration, conservation, and sustainable use represent distinct typologies, they are interconnected and often complement one another in NBS projects. For example, a watershed management initiative might involve restoring degraded riparian zones, conserving upstream forests, and promoting sustainable agricultural practices downstream. This integrated approach maximizes the benefits of each typology, addressing multiple challenges simultaneously.

The choice of typology depends on the specific context and objectives of the project. Restoration is often prioritized in areas with severe ecosystem degradation, while conservation is critical for safeguarding pristine environments. Sustainable use is ideal for balancing ecological and socio-economic needs in regions with high resource dependency. In many cases, a combination of these typologies is necessary to achieve long-term sustainability and resilience.

Summary

The typologies of restoration, conservation, and sustainable use form the foundation of NBS, offering diverse approaches to enhance ecosystem health and address societal challenges. Restoration focuses on reversing degradation, conservation ensures the protection of intact ecosystems, and sustainable use promotes resource management that balances environmental and economic needs. Together, these typologies provide a flexible and holistic framework for designing and implementing NBS projects that contribute to climate resilience, biodiversity conservation, and sustainable development.

Linking PES and NBS to the Sustainable Development Goals

The Sustainable Development Goals (SDGs), established by the United Nations in 2015, provide a global framework for addressing pressing environmental, social, and economic challenges by 2030. Both PES and NBS contribute directly to achieving the SDGs by aligning ecological conservation with economic incentives and sustainable development strategies. Together, PES and NBS bridge critical gaps between environmental stewardship, poverty alleviation, and climate resilience, advancing the interconnected nature of the SDGs.

SDG 13: Climate Action

PES schemes support NBS projects such as reforestation, wetland restoration, and sustainable land management, which play a vital role in mitigating climate change by sequestering carbon and enhancing ecosystem resilience. For example, PES payments incentivize farmers to adopt agroforestry practices that increase carbon storage while improving soil health. By financing these climate-focused NBS, PES accelerates progress toward SDG 13, promoting adaptation and mitigation strategies in vulnerable regions.

SDG 6: Clean Water and Sanitation

NBS initiatives that restore wetlands, protect watersheds, or manage forests contribute to water purification, groundwater recharge, and flood regulation. PES facilitates these efforts by compensating stakeholders for practices that maintain or enhance water-related ecosystem services. For instance, downstream water users can finance PES schemes to incentivize upstream communities to protect forested areas, ensuring clean and reliable water supplies. This alignment with SDG 6 underscores the role of PES in addressing water security and improving access to clean water.

SDG 15: Life on Land

PES schemes directly support NBS aimed at conserving terrestrial ecosystems and halting biodiversity loss, aligning with SDG 15. Protected areas, reforestation projects, and habitat restoration efforts are often financed through PES mechanisms, rewarding stakeholders for preserving critical ecosystems. By encouraging landowners to adopt conservation practices, PES enhances biodiversity, combats desertification, and fosters sustainable land use.

SDG 1: No Poverty and SDG 8: Decent Work and Economic Growth

PES schemes create economic opportunities by rewarding communities and individuals for their role in ecosystem management. Payments provide an alternative income source, particularly for rural and marginalized groups, reducing poverty (SDG 1) and promoting sustainable livelihoods (SDG 8). By integrating PES into NBS projects, such as sustainable agriculture and forestry, economic benefits are coupled with environmental gains.

SDG 11: Sustainable Cities and Communities

Urban-focused NBS, such as green roofs, urban forests, and floodplain restoration, contribute to more sustainable and resilient cities. PES can finance these initiatives by incentivizing stakeholders, such as private developers or local governments, to invest in urban NBS that improve air quality, reduce urban heat islands, and mitigate flood risks. This supports SDG 11 by enhancing the livability and resilience of urban areas.

Synergies Across Goals

The integration of PES and NBS fosters synergies across multiple SDGs by addressing interconnected challenges. For example, a PES-funded reforestation project can simultaneously advance SDG 13 (climate action), SDG 15 (life on land), and SDG 1 (poverty reduction) by enhancing carbon sequestration, conserving biodiversity, and providing income to local communities. This holistic approach reflects the mutually reinforcing nature of the SDGs.

Summary

PES and NBS are powerful tools for achieving the SDGs, bridging environmental conservation with sustainable development. By incentivizing practices that enhance ecosystem services, PES ensures the financial sustainability of NBS projects, directly contributing to goals such as climate action, water security, and poverty alleviation. Together, they provide a pathway for integrated, scalable solutions to global challenges.

Chapter 2: Designing PES Schemes for NBS

Designing effective PES schemes to support NBS requires careful planning, stakeholder engagement, and alignment with ecological, social, and economic goals. A well-designed PES scheme ensures that financial incentives drive measurable outcomes, such as enhanced ecosystem services and increased sustainability. This chapter explores the key components of PES scheme design, including identifying ecosystem services, establishing baselines, structuring payments, and addressing challenges such as valuation and equity. By focusing on practical considerations and strategies, this chapter provides a roadmap for creating PES schemes that effectively finance and scale NBS initiatives.

Essential Components of PES Schemes: Identifying Buyers, Sellers, and Ecosystem Services

A PES scheme is built on a foundational structure involving buyers, sellers, and the ecosystem services they transact. These components must be clearly identified and well-defined to ensure the effectiveness, transparency, and sustainability of the scheme. Each component plays a critical role in aligning incentives, delivering measurable outcomes, and maintaining trust among participants.

Identifying Buyers

Buyers are the beneficiaries of ecosystem services who are willing to pay for their continued provision or enhancement. These can include individuals, businesses, governments, or non-governmental organizations (NGOs). The motivations for buyers vary but generally fall into three categories:

1. **Private Sector Buyers**: Companies may participate in PES schemes to offset environmental impacts, meet corporate social responsibility (CSR) goals, or secure critical resources for their

operations. For instance, a beverage company might invest in watershed protection to ensure clean and reliable water supplies for production.

2. **Public Sector Buyers**: Governments often act as buyers to achieve broader environmental or social objectives, such as carbon sequestration, biodiversity conservation, or water quality improvement. Public funding for PES can come from environmental taxes, green bonds, or budget allocations.

3. **Voluntary Buyers**: NGOs, philanthropic organizations, or individuals may contribute to PES schemes out of a commitment to conservation or social equity. For example, an environmental NGO might fund reforestation projects to combat climate change.

Buyers must perceive a clear value in the ecosystem services provided and have confidence that their investments will lead to the desired outcomes. This requires effective communication of benefits and robust mechanisms for monitoring and reporting.

Identifying Sellers

Sellers are the providers of ecosystem services, typically individuals, communities, or organizations who own, manage, or influence the ecosystems in question. Sellers agree to undertake specific actions, such as conservation, restoration, or sustainable resource management, in exchange for payments.

1. **Individual Landowners**: Farmers, foresters, or other private landholders are common participants in PES schemes. They may adopt practices like reforestation, agroforestry, or soil conservation to deliver ecosystem services.

2. **Communities**: In many cases, indigenous or rural communities manage ecosystems collectively. PES schemes targeting these

groups often focus on equitable benefit-sharing and capacity-building to ensure active participation.

3. **Public Agencies**: Publicly managed lands, such as national parks or forests, can also act as sellers. In these cases, PES payments might fund conservation programs or operational costs.

To ensure the scheme's success, sellers must have clear incentives to participate. Payments should outweigh the opportunity costs of alternative land uses, and the terms of engagement must be fair, transparent, and contextually appropriate.

Identifying Ecosystem Services

Ecosystem services are the benefits derived from ecosystems, which form the basis of PES transactions. Identifying the specific services to be conserved or enhanced is crucial for designing a targeted and effective PES scheme. These services are typically categorized into four groups:

1. **Provisioning Services**: These include tangible goods such as water, food, timber, and medicinal resources. For example, a PES scheme might compensate a community for sustainable forestry practices that maintain timber supplies while preserving biodiversity.

2. **Regulating Services**: These involve natural processes that control environmental conditions, such as carbon sequestration, flood regulation, and water purification. A PES scheme for watershed management, for instance, may focus on restoring wetlands to improve water quality and reduce flood risks.

3. **Cultural Services**: These are non-material benefits, including recreation, aesthetic value, and cultural heritage. PES schemes targeting these services might include payments to maintain landscapes that attract tourism or preserve cultural sites.

4. **Supporting Services**: These are underlying processes, such as nutrient cycling and soil formation, that enable other ecosystem services. While often indirect, supporting services are vital to the long-term sustainability of PES schemes.

Defining ecosystem services requires baseline assessments to determine their current state, potential improvements, and measurable outcomes. Clear metrics and monitoring mechanisms are essential to ensure that the identified services are being maintained or enhanced as agreed.

Summary

The success of a PES scheme relies on clearly identifying and aligning buyers, sellers, and the ecosystem services being transacted. Buyers must perceive value in the services they pay for, sellers must be incentivized to provide those services, and the targeted ecosystem services must be well-defined, measurable, and meaningful. By establishing these components with clarity and precision, PES schemes can effectively incentivize conservation, restoration, and sustainable use, driving long-term environmental and social benefits.

Setting Baselines and Ensuring Conditionality

Setting baselines and ensuring conditionality are critical components of PES schemes. These elements establish the foundation for measuring progress, determining payments, and ensuring accountability in delivering ecosystem services. Without clear baselines and well-defined conditionality, PES schemes risk failing to achieve their intended environmental and social outcomes.

Setting Baselines

A baseline represents the current state of an ecosystem and its associated services before the implementation of a PES scheme. It provides a reference point against which changes can be measured, enabling the assessment of whether the scheme delivers additional benefits. Establishing baselines involves evaluating ecological, social, and economic conditions to determine what would likely happen in the absence of the PES intervention.

1. **Defining the Current State**: Baselines capture key metrics, such as forest cover, carbon stocks, water quality, or species diversity. For example, a PES scheme aimed at reforestation would document the extent of degraded land and its current carbon storage capacity.

2. **Determining the Business-as-Usual (BAU) Scenario**: The BAU scenario predicts how ecosystems and their services would evolve without PES intervention. This step is crucial for establishing additionality—the principle that PES schemes should deliver benefits beyond what would occur naturally or under existing policies.

3. **Using Scientific and Local Knowledge**: Baselines are established using a combination of scientific data, such as satellite imagery and ecological surveys, and local knowledge provided by communities and stakeholders. This ensures accuracy and relevance to the specific context.

4. **Adapting Over Time**: Ecosystems are dynamic, and baselines may need adjustments to reflect changing conditions or new information. PES schemes should include mechanisms for updating baselines periodically to maintain their validity and usefulness.

Ensuring Conditionality

Conditionality is a defining characteristic of PES schemes. It links payments directly to the achievement of specific environmental outcomes or the implementation of agreed-upon actions. This principle ensures that financial resources are used effectively and that stakeholders are accountable for their commitments.

1. **Defining Performance Metrics**: Conditionality requires clear, measurable indicators of success. For example, a PES scheme focused on water quality improvement might track reductions in sediment levels or nutrient concentrations.

2. **Establishing Monitoring and Verification Systems**: Regular monitoring ensures that participants meet the conditions of the PES agreement. Verification processes, such as on-site inspections or remote sensing, confirm that the ecosystem services are being delivered as agreed.

3. **Payment Triggers**: Payments are disbursed only when the conditions are met. For example, landowners might receive compensation after demonstrating that forest cover has been maintained or increased over a specified period.

4. **Balancing Flexibility and Rigor**: While conditionality must be robust, it should also accommodate unforeseen circumstances. For instance, natural disasters or external pressures may affect participants' ability to meet their obligations. PES schemes should include provisions for addressing such situations without compromising their integrity.

The Interdependence of Baselines and Conditionality

Baselines and conditionality are closely linked. Baselines provide the reference point needed to define the conditions for payments, while conditionality ensures that participants deliver benefits above the baseline. Together, they create a transparent and accountable framework for PES schemes, enabling stakeholders to track progress, allocate resources efficiently, and build trust.

Summary

Setting baselines and ensuring conditionality are essential for the success of PES schemes. Baselines establish a clear starting point for measuring additionality, while conditionality guarantees that payments are tied to tangible outcomes. By integrating these components effectively, PES schemes can deliver measurable and lasting benefits for ecosystems and the communities that depend on them.

Valuation of Ecosystem Services: Economic, Social, and Ecological Perspectives

Valuing ecosystem services is a critical step in designing PES schemes. Accurate valuation helps quantify the benefits ecosystems provide, establish the basis for payments, and justify investments in conservation, restoration, or sustainable use. Ecosystem services can be valued from three interrelated perspectives: economic, social, and ecological. Each perspective offers unique insights that collectively ensure the holistic design and implementation of PES schemes.

Economic Valuation

Economic valuation seeks to assign monetary value to ecosystem services by estimating the direct and indirect benefits they provide. This perspective helps stakeholders understand the financial implications of ecosystem conservation or degradation, enabling decision-makers to allocate resources effectively.

1. **Market-Based Valuation**: For provisioning services, such as timber, water, or fish, market prices are often used as proxies for value. For instance, the value of clean water in a PES scheme might be based on the costs avoided by not having to invest in water treatment facilities.

2. **Non-Market Valuation**: Many ecosystem services, particularly regulating and cultural services, do not have direct market prices. Techniques such as contingent valuation (willingness to pay) and hedonic pricing (value reflected in property prices) are used to estimate their economic worth. For example, the flood regulation service of wetlands can be valued based on the avoided damage costs from floods.

3. **Cost-Benefit Analysis (CBA)**: Economic valuation often includes CBA to compare the costs of implementing a PES scheme with the financial benefits derived from the ecosystem services it supports. This analysis helps demonstrate the financial feasibility and efficiency of PES initiatives.

While economic valuation is crucial, it can oversimplify the complexity of ecosystems by reducing them to monetary terms. To address this, it should be complemented by social and ecological valuation methods.

Social Valuation

Social valuation emphasizes the non-monetary benefits ecosystems provide to individuals and communities, such as cultural heritage, recreational opportunities, and spiritual significance. This perspective highlights the role of ecosystems in supporting social well-being and cohesion.

1. **Cultural and Spiritual Values**: Many ecosystems hold intrinsic value for communities due to their cultural and spiritual significance. For instance, sacred groves or culturally important landscapes may be central to the identity and practices of indigenous peoples. While these values are difficult to monetize, they are crucial for the design of PES schemes that respect cultural heritage.

2. **Recreational and Educational Benefits**: Ecosystems often provide recreational spaces and educational opportunities. Parks, forests, and wetlands are used for leisure, tourism, and learning, contributing to physical and mental well-being. PES schemes may incorporate these social benefits to enhance community engagement and support.

3. **Equity and Livelihood Considerations**: Social valuation includes assessing how ecosystem services contribute to livelihoods, particularly for marginalized or resource-dependent communities.

For example, agroforestry systems supported by PES schemes can improve food security and income while preserving biodiversity.

Social valuation ensures that PES schemes are inclusive and equitable, addressing the needs and priorities of all stakeholders. It emphasizes the importance of participatory approaches to capture diverse values and perspectives.

Ecological Valuation

Ecological valuation focuses on the intrinsic and functional value of ecosystems, independent of their direct benefits to humans. It emphasizes the role of ecosystems in maintaining biodiversity, ecological processes, and planetary health.

1. **Biodiversity Value**: Healthy ecosystems with high biodiversity are more resilient and capable of providing a wide range of services. For instance, diverse forests are better at carbon sequestration, water regulation, and habitat provision. Ecological valuation highlights the importance of conserving species and genetic diversity as a foundation for ecosystem services.

2. **Functional Value**: This approach considers the ecological processes that sustain ecosystems, such as nutrient cycling, pollination, and soil formation. For example, wetlands provide essential functions like water filtration and habitat connectivity, which are critical for ecosystem stability.

3. **Intrinsic Value**: Ecological valuation recognizes that ecosystems have value in and of themselves, regardless of their utility to humans. This perspective aligns with ethical and conservation principles, emphasizing the moral responsibility to protect nature for its own sake.

Ecological valuation complements economic and social approaches by highlighting the long-term benefits of maintaining ecosystem health. It ensures that PES schemes are designed to preserve ecological integrity and sustainability.

Integration of Perspectives

An effective valuation process integrates economic, social, and ecological perspectives to capture the full range of ecosystem benefits. For example, a PES scheme for forest conservation might combine economic valuation (timber revenue), social valuation (recreational and cultural importance), and ecological valuation (biodiversity and carbon sequestration). This multi-dimensional approach ensures that PES schemes reflect the true value of ecosystems, fostering buy-in from diverse stakeholders.

Valuation methods should also be context-specific, considering the unique characteristics of ecosystems and the priorities of local communities. Participatory approaches, where stakeholders contribute to the valuation process, enhance accuracy and legitimacy.

Challenges in Valuation

Valuing ecosystem services is not without challenges. The complexity of ecosystems makes it difficult to fully capture their value, particularly for non-market services and intrinsic ecological functions. Additionally, biases in economic methods can undervalue cultural and ecological benefits, while social and ecological approaches may lack quantifiable metrics. Balancing these challenges requires adopting transparent, inclusive, and adaptive valuation methods.

Summary

The valuation of ecosystem services is essential for designing PES schemes that effectively support conservation, restoration, and sustainable use. By combining economic, social, and ecological perspectives, stakeholders can capture the multifaceted benefits of ecosystems, ensuring that PES schemes are equitable, sustainable, and impactful. This integrated approach not only strengthens the design and implementation of PES but also highlights the critical role of ecosystems in supporting life, livelihoods, and resilience.

Structuring Payments: Monetary and Non-Monetary Rewards

In PES schemes, structuring payments is a critical step that directly influences participation, compliance, and the success of the initiative. Payments can be designed as monetary or non-monetary rewards, depending on the goals of the scheme, the preferences of participants, and the socio-economic context. A well-structured payment system ensures that ecosystem service providers are adequately incentivized while fostering long-term sustainability.

Monetary Rewards

Monetary payments are the most common form of compensation in PES schemes, providing direct financial incentives to participants. These payments are typically structured based on the value of the ecosystem services provided, the costs incurred by service providers, and the opportunity costs of alternative land uses.

1. **Fixed Payments**: In some schemes, participants receive a predetermined amount for their participation. For example, landowners might be paid a fixed annual fee for maintaining forest cover or adopting sustainable agricultural practices.

2. **Performance-Based Payments**: Payments can be tied to measurable outcomes, such as the amount of carbon sequestered, improvements in water quality, or increases in biodiversity. Performance-based payments ensure accountability and link compensation directly to results.

3. **Tiered Payments**: In tiered systems, payments vary based on the level of service provided or the importance of the ecosystem. For instance, higher payments might be allocated for preserving critical habitats compared to less sensitive areas.

Monetary rewards are straightforward and effective, particularly in regions where financial incentives directly impact livelihood decisions. However, they must be carefully calibrated to ensure fairness and sustainability.

Non-Monetary Rewards

Non-monetary rewards provide indirect incentives that benefit participants without direct financial compensation. These rewards can be equally effective, particularly in contexts where financial payments may not align with cultural norms or long-term objectives.

1. **Capacity-Building**: PES schemes may offer training, technical support, or access to resources that enhance participants' ability to manage ecosystems sustainably. For example, farmers might receive training in agroforestry or soil conservation techniques.

2. **Access to Markets**: In some cases, participants are given access to premium markets for sustainably produced goods. For instance, certification schemes for eco-friendly products can increase market value and provide indirect economic benefits.

3. **Community Benefits**: Non-monetary rewards can also include investments in community infrastructure, such as schools, healthcare facilities, or water systems, which benefit the entire community and build support for the PES scheme.

Summary

Structuring payments in PES schemes requires balancing monetary and non-monetary rewards to align with participants' needs and the scheme's goals. Monetary payments offer direct financial incentives, while non-monetary rewards provide long-term benefits that strengthen capacity and community well-being. Combining these approaches ensures that PES schemes are inclusive, sustainable, and effective in achieving environmental objectives.

Challenges and Solutions in Designing PES for NBS

Designing PES schemes to support NBS involves several challenges, but these can be addressed with thoughtful planning and innovative solutions.

One major challenge is valuing ecosystem services, especially non-market benefits like biodiversity or cultural significance. Accurate valuation requires robust scientific data and participatory approaches to capture the full range of ecosystem benefits. Tools like cost-benefit analysis and willingness-to-pay surveys can help estimate these values.

Another issue is ensuring additionality, where PES must deliver benefits beyond what would occur without intervention. Baseline assessments and clearly defined metrics are essential to demonstrate the additional value generated by the scheme.

Equitable benefit-sharing poses another challenge, particularly when involving marginalized communities or indigenous groups. Inclusive decision-making, transparent agreements, and fair compensation mechanisms can ensure all stakeholders benefit.

Monitoring and enforcement can also be complex, especially in remote areas. Technology like remote sensing and geospatial tools can improve monitoring efficiency, while community-based approaches can enhance enforcement.

Lastly, long-term financial sustainability is critical for scaling NBS. Blended financing, combining public, private, and philanthropic funds, can provide reliable resources for PES schemes.

By addressing these challenges with targeted solutions, PES schemes can effectively support NBS, ensuring ecological, social, and economic resilience.

Chapter 3: Governance and Institutional Frameworks for PES in NBS

Governance and institutional frameworks play a critical role in the successful implementation of PES schemes, particularly in supporting NBS. Effective governance ensures transparency, accountability, and equitable participation, while robust institutional arrangements provide the legal, regulatory, and operational foundation needed to sustain PES initiatives. This chapter explores the key elements of governance and institutional design, including public, private, and hybrid governance models, legal frameworks, and mechanisms for ensuring benefit-sharing and compliance. By examining these aspects, the chapter highlights how strong governance and institutional support are essential for aligning PES schemes with NBS goals and achieving long-term environmental and social outcomes.

Governance Models: Public, Private, and Hybrid Approaches

Governance models play a critical role in shaping PES schemes and their alignment with NBS. Effective governance ensures that PES schemes are transparent, accountable, and inclusive, fostering trust among stakeholders and supporting long-term sustainability. The governance of PES schemes can take various forms, including public, private, and hybrid approaches, each with distinct characteristics, strengths, and challenges.

Public Governance Models

In public governance models, governments or public institutions take the lead in designing, implementing, and managing PES schemes. These models are often used to address large-scale environmental issues, such as climate change, water security, and biodiversity conservation, that require coordinated efforts and significant funding.

1. **Strengths**:

• Public governance can leverage regulatory frameworks, such as environmental laws and land-use policies, to enforce compliance and ensure accountability.

• Governments often have access to large funding pools, sourced from environmental taxes, public budgets, or international aid.

• Publicly governed PES schemes can target public goods, such as clean air or water, ensuring widespread benefits.

2. **Challenges**:

• Bureaucratic inefficiencies and limited resources may delay implementation or reduce the effectiveness of PES schemes.

• Ensuring equitable benefit distribution and community participation can be challenging in top-down governance structures.

Examples of public governance include national reforestation programs or watershed management initiatives funded by government agencies.

Private Governance Models

Private governance models are led by corporations, NGOs, or other private entities. These models are typically market-driven, with private sector stakeholders acting as both buyers and facilitators of ecosystem services.

1. **Strengths**:

• Private governance models are often more flexible and innovative, adapting quickly to changing circumstances or market opportunities.

• They can target specific ecosystem services that align with CSR or business goals, such as carbon offsets or water stewardship.

• Private models often foster strong partnerships with local communities, ensuring tailored solutions.

2. **Challenges**:

• Profit-driven motives may prioritize short-term gains over long-term environmental sustainability.

• Private governance can exclude marginalized communities if not carefully designed, leading to inequitable outcomes.

For instance, a beverage company might fund a PES scheme to incentivize upstream landowners to adopt sustainable farming practices that protect water quality.

Hybrid Governance Models

Hybrid governance models combine public and private efforts, leveraging the strengths of both sectors to create more effective and inclusive PES schemes. These models often involve collaborations between governments, businesses, NGOs, and local communities.

1. **Strengths**:

• Hybrid models integrate the regulatory authority of public institutions with the innovation and efficiency of the private sector.

• They are well-suited for addressing complex challenges that require multi-stakeholder engagement, such as climate resilience or landscape restoration.

• By pooling resources and expertise, hybrid models can achieve greater scale and impact.

2. **Challenges**:

• Coordinating diverse stakeholders can be time-consuming and resource-intensive.

• Conflicting priorities between public and private actors may complicate decision-making and implementation.

Examples of hybrid governance include public-private partnerships for forest conservation, where government agencies set regulatory frameworks while private companies provide funding and expertise.

Comparative Insights

Each governance model has unique advantages and limitations, making the choice of model context-dependent. Public governance is often better suited for addressing large-scale public goods, while private models excel in targeted, market-driven initiatives. Hybrid models offer a balance, enabling collaboration across sectors to achieve broader goals. The success of any governance model depends on its ability to ensure transparency, inclusivity, and accountability while fostering trust among stakeholders.

Summary

Governance models are foundational to the success of PES schemes in supporting NBS. Public, private, and hybrid approaches each bring unique strengths to the table, offering flexibility to address diverse environmental and social challenges. By selecting the appropriate governance model and adapting it to the local context, PES schemes can effectively align conservation efforts with sustainable development goals, ensuring long-term ecological and societal benefits.

Institutional Structures for PES Scheme Management: Rules, Regulations, and Enforcement

Institutional structures are critical for the successful implementation and sustainability of PES schemes. They provide the framework within which PES schemes operate, ensuring that rules are established, regulations are enforced, and participants adhere to their commitments. Effective institutional structures promote transparency, accountability, and equity, creating an environment where ecosystem services can be managed and financed sustainably.

Rules for PES Schemes

Rules form the foundation of PES schemes, defining the roles, responsibilities, and expectations of all participants. Clear and enforceable rules are essential to ensure compliance, build trust among stakeholders, and facilitate the smooth functioning of the scheme.

1. **Defining Participation**: Rules establish eligibility criteria for buyers and sellers, specifying who can participate and under what conditions. For example, landowners may need to demonstrate land tenure or the ability to provide specific ecosystem services.

2. **Performance Metrics**: Clear guidelines are set for the ecosystem services to be provided, including measurable indicators such as carbon sequestration rates, water quality improvements, or biodiversity levels.

3. **Payment Terms**: Rules outline how payments will be structured, including the amount, frequency, and conditions under which payments will be made.

4. **Conflict Resolution**: Effective rules include mechanisms for addressing disputes, ensuring that conflicts among participants or

between stakeholders and administrators can be resolved fairly and efficiently.

Regulations for PES Schemes

Regulations are formal policies or legal frameworks that provide the overarching guidance for PES schemes. They ensure that PES schemes align with national or regional environmental goals, legal requirements, and international commitments.

1. **Legal Recognition**: Institutional regulations provide the legal foundation for PES schemes, clarifying property rights, land tenure, and the ownership of ecosystem services. Secure land tenure is particularly critical for ensuring that participants, especially marginalized communities, can benefit from PES schemes without fear of displacement or exploitation.

2. **Environmental Standards**: Regulations define the minimum standards for ecosystem services, ensuring that PES schemes contribute to broader environmental objectives, such as biodiversity conservation, climate resilience, or water security.

3. **Alignment with Policies**: PES schemes are often integrated into broader policy frameworks, such as climate action plans, sustainable development strategies, or agricultural policies. This alignment ensures coherence and maximizes the impact of PES initiatives.

4. **Transparency Requirements**: Regulatory frameworks often mandate transparent reporting and monitoring practices to prevent misuse of funds and ensure accountability to all stakeholders.

Enforcement in PES Schemes

Enforcement mechanisms ensure that the rules and regulations governing PES schemes are followed, and violations are addressed promptly. Effective enforcement builds trust and confidence among participants and ensures that the desired ecosystem services are delivered.

1. **Monitoring and Verification**: Regular monitoring of ecosystem services is essential for verifying compliance. Tools such as remote sensing, field surveys, and geospatial analysis are commonly used to track changes in ecosystem conditions.

2. **Compliance Audits**: Periodic audits ensure that participants meet their obligations and that payments are tied to actual performance. Audits can be conducted by independent third parties to enhance credibility.

3. **Penalties and Incentives**: Enforcement mechanisms often include penalties for non-compliance, such as payment reductions, contract termination, or legal actions. Conversely, additional incentives may be offered for exceeding performance targets.

4. **Community-Based Enforcement**: In many cases, local communities play a key role in monitoring and enforcing PES agreements. Community-based enforcement can be particularly effective in building local ownership and reducing administrative costs.

Challenges in Institutional Structures

Despite their importance, institutional structures face several challenges in managing PES schemes effectively. These include inadequate capacity for monitoring and enforcement, conflicting regulations across sectors, and power imbalances that marginalize vulnerable groups. Addressing these challenges requires capacity-building, adaptive management, and participatory governance.

Summary

Institutional structures, encompassing rules, regulations, and enforcement mechanisms, are essential for the effective management of PES schemes. By providing clarity, accountability, and transparency, these structures ensure that PES initiatives deliver measurable environmental benefits while fostering trust and equity among stakeholders. Strong institutional frameworks are therefore critical for scaling PES schemes to support NBS and achieve broader sustainability goals.

Legal and Policy Frameworks Supporting PES-NBS Integration

The successful implementation and scaling of PES schemes to support NBS rely on robust legal and policy frameworks. These frameworks provide the structural foundation to legitimize PES schemes, align them with broader sustainability goals, and ensure equity, transparency, and accountability. By addressing issues such as property rights, environmental regulations, and cross-sectoral policies, legal and policy frameworks play a crucial role in integrating PES with NBS.

Establishing Legal Foundations for PES

1. Property Rights and Land Tenure

Clear property rights are fundamental to PES schemes, as they define who owns or manages the land and ecosystem services. Secure land tenure ensures that service providers, such as landowners or communities, have the authority to enter into PES agreements and benefit from them. Ambiguities in land tenure can lead to conflicts, discourage participation, and undermine the scheme's credibility. Legal frameworks must therefore address land tenure issues, particularly in regions with communal or customary land ownership systems.

2. Ecosystem Service Ownership

Laws that define the ownership of ecosystem services, such as carbon storage, water purification, or biodiversity, are essential for PES schemes. For instance, carbon sequestration credits must be legally recognized for PES schemes involving reforestation or forest conservation. Legal clarity prevents disputes over who can claim payments for ecosystem services and ensures the scheme operates within a legitimate framework.

3. Contractual Agreements

PES schemes depend on enforceable contracts between buyers and sellers of ecosystem services. Legal frameworks should standardize contract terms, ensuring that agreements are transparent, fair, and enforceable. Contracts should include provisions for monitoring, penalties for non-compliance, and mechanisms for dispute resolution.

Policy Alignment with PES and NBS

1. Integration with National Development Strategies

PES schemes are most effective when aligned with national development goals and environmental policies. For instance, countries implementing climate action plans under the Paris Agreement can integrate PES as a tool for achieving nationally determined contributions (NDCs). Similarly, PES schemes can support biodiversity targets under the Convention on Biological Diversity (CBD) or water security goals in national adaptation plans.

2. Environmental Regulations

Environmental laws, such as those governing protected areas, water management, or forest conservation, provide a policy framework for PES schemes. For example, water use regulations can mandate payments from downstream users to upstream communities for watershed protection. Legal instruments that enforce ecosystem protection can also complement voluntary PES schemes, creating a dual approach to conservation.

3. Cross-Sectoral Coordination

PES schemes often intersect with policies in agriculture, forestry, water management, and urban planning. Policy coherence across these sectors is essential to avoid conflicts and enhance the efficiency of PES schemes. For instance, agricultural policies promoting sustainable farming practices can align with PES initiatives that incentivize soil conservation or agroforestry.

4. Incentive Structures

Policies that provide tax benefits, subsidies, or other incentives for ecosystem service buyers can enhance participation in PES schemes. For example, tax breaks for companies investing in carbon credits or biodiversity offsets can create financial incentives for private sector engagement in NBS projects.

International and Regional Frameworks

1. Global Agreements

International agreements, such as the Paris Agreement and the Sustainable Development Goals (SDGs), create a supportive environment for PES and NBS integration. These frameworks encourage countries to adopt innovative financing mechanisms, including PES, to achieve climate, biodiversity, and sustainability targets. Multilateral initiatives like REDD+ (Reducing Emissions from Deforestation and Forest Degradation) provide a global platform for PES schemes focused on forest conservation.

2. Regional Cooperation

Regional frameworks, such as the European Union's Green Deal or Africa's Great Green Wall Initiative, support the integration of PES with NBS at a transboundary scale. These initiatives provide policy guidance, funding opportunities, and technical assistance for implementing PES schemes that address shared environmental challenges.

Addressing Challenges in Legal and Policy Frameworks

Despite their importance, legal and policy frameworks for PES-NBS integration face several challenges:

1. **Regulatory Gaps**

In many regions, laws and policies do not explicitly address PES or ecosystem service markets, leading to uncertainty and limiting the scalability of schemes. Governments need to develop targeted policies that recognize and support PES initiatives.

2. **Equity and Inclusion**

Legal and policy frameworks must ensure that marginalized communities, such as indigenous peoples or small-scale farmers, are not excluded from PES benefits. Inclusive policies that protect their rights and provide capacity-building support are essential for equitable outcomes.

3. **Policy Fragmentation**

Inconsistent policies across sectors or levels of government can create barriers to PES-NBS integration. Coordinated policy-making and cross-sectoral collaboration are crucial to overcome fragmentation.

Summary

Legal and policy frameworks are indispensable for integrating PES and NBS, providing the structural foundation for their design, implementation, and scalability. By addressing property rights, aligning with national and international goals, and ensuring policy coherence, these frameworks enable PES schemes to deliver measurable environmental and social benefits. Strengthening legal and policy support for PES-NBS integration is key to achieving long-term sustainability and resilience in the face of global environmental challenges.

Ensuring Transparency, Accountability, and Equitable Benefit-Sharing

Transparency, accountability, and equitable benefit-sharing are essential principles in the design and implementation of PES schemes. These elements not only foster trust and cooperation among stakeholders but also ensure that the schemes achieve their intended environmental and social objectives. When effectively applied, they enhance the credibility, inclusivity, and sustainability of PES initiatives, particularly when integrated with NBS.

Transparency

Transparency ensures that information about the design, implementation, and outcomes of PES schemes is accessible and understandable to all stakeholders. It promotes fairness, reduces misunderstandings, and builds trust in the process.

1. **Clear Objectives**: PES schemes must define and communicate their goals explicitly, such as biodiversity conservation, carbon sequestration, or water quality improvement. Clear objectives guide all participants and provide a basis for evaluating success.

2. **Accessible Information**: Stakeholders should have access to all relevant information, including contract terms, payment structures, performance indicators, and monitoring processes. This openness

ensures that participants can make informed decisions and understand their roles.

3. **Participatory Processes**: Transparency is enhanced when stakeholders are involved in key decisions, such as setting payment rates or defining performance metrics. Regular consultations and open dialogues enable diverse perspectives to shape the scheme.

4. **Public Reporting**: Sharing regular updates and reports on financial flows, ecological impacts, and participant compliance increases confidence in the scheme. Publicly available data also supports external evaluations and fosters accountability.

Accountability

Accountability ensures that all parties adhere to their commitments and that resources are used effectively. It requires robust systems for monitoring, evaluation, and enforcement to ensure that ecosystem services are delivered as promised.

1. **Monitoring Performance**: Regular and systematic monitoring of ecosystem services is vital. For example, forest cover in a reforestation project can be tracked using satellite imagery, while water quality improvements can be assessed through field testing.

2. **Verification and Audits**: Independent third-party verification of outcomes enhances accountability by providing unbiased assessments. Audits ensure that payments are tied to actual performance and help detect discrepancies or non-compliance.

3. **Contractual Clarity**: Detailed agreements outline the roles and responsibilities of each participant, including penalties for failing to meet obligations. For instance, payments may be withheld or adjusted if service providers do not achieve agreed-upon targets.

4. **Grievance Mechanisms**: Dispute resolution systems, such as mediation or arbitration, allow stakeholders to address conflicts efficiently and fairly. Accessible grievance mechanisms promote trust and reduce the risk of disputes escalating.

Equitable Benefit-Sharing

Equitable benefit-sharing ensures that the financial and non-financial rewards from PES schemes are distributed fairly among all participants, especially vulnerable or marginalized groups. It supports social inclusion and minimizes conflicts over resources.

1. **Fair Payments**: Compensation should reflect the opportunity costs incurred by service providers, such as income forgone from alternative land uses. Payments must be adequate to incentivize participation and maintain sustainability.

2. **Inclusivity**: Inclusive schemes involve all relevant stakeholders, such as smallholder farmers, indigenous communities, and women, ensuring that the benefits reach those most dependent on ecosystem services.

3. **Capacity-Building**: Equitable participation often requires investments in capacity-building, such as training, technical assistance, or access to financial resources. These efforts empower marginalized groups to engage effectively in PES schemes.

4. **Community Benefits**: Beyond individual payments, PES schemes can deliver broader community-level benefits, such as improved infrastructure, education, or healthcare. These collective benefits enhance local support and contribute to long-term development.

Challenges and Solutions

Ensuring transparency, accountability, and equitable benefit-sharing in PES schemes can be challenging. Common barriers include power imbalances, limited institutional capacity, and high monitoring costs.

1. **Addressing Power Dynamics**: Establishing participatory governance structures and legal safeguards helps ensure that all voices, particularly those of marginalized groups, are heard and respected.

2. **Strengthening Capacity**: Building the institutional and technical capacity of stakeholders supports effective implementation, monitoring, and equitable distribution of benefits.

3. **Reducing Costs**: The use of digital tools, such as remote sensing and automated reporting platforms, can lower the costs of monitoring and verification while maintaining accuracy and transparency.

Summary

Transparency, accountability, and equitable benefit-sharing are foundational principles for the success of PES schemes. By prioritizing these elements, PES initiatives can foster trust, ensure fairness, and achieve meaningful environmental and social outcomes. Strengthening these principles is vital for the integration of PES with NBS, driving inclusive and sustainable development that benefits both ecosystems and communities.

Chapter 4: Financing Mechanisms for PES and NBS

Financing is a critical factor in the successful implementation and scaling of PES schemes and NBS. Effective financing mechanisms ensure that sufficient resources are mobilized to support ecosystem service providers, cover operational costs, and deliver long-term environmental and social benefits. This chapter explores the diverse financing mechanisms that underpin PES schemes, including public funding, private sector contributions, and blended finance approaches. It also examines innovative financial instruments such as carbon markets, green bonds, and environmental taxes, highlighting their potential to drive investments in NBS. By addressing the challenges and opportunities associated with financing PES schemes, the chapter provides a comprehensive framework for developing sustainable and scalable funding models.

Overview of PES Financing Models: Public, Private, and Blended Approaches

Effective financing models are essential for the successful implementation and sustainability of PES schemes. These models provide the resources needed to incentivize ecosystem service providers, support operational activities, and scale initiatives. PES financing typically falls into three main categories: public, private, and blended approaches. Each model offers unique advantages and challenges, and the choice often depends on the objectives, scale, and context of the scheme.

Public Financing Models

Public financing models rely on government funding or resources from international development organizations. These models are particularly suited to large-scale PES schemes that deliver public goods, such as biodiversity conservation, watershed protection, and climate change mitigation.

1. Government Funding

Governments play a significant role in financing PES schemes through budget allocations, environmental taxes, or revenues from natural resource extraction. For example, national reforestation programs may be funded through general tax revenues or earmarked funds such as carbon taxes. Public financing ensures stability and predictability, making it easier to implement long-term PES initiatives.

2. International Development Support

Multilateral and bilateral development agencies, such as the United Nations or the World Bank, often provide grants or loans for PES schemes. These funds typically support projects aligned with global environmental goals, such as climate resilience or biodiversity conservation. For instance, the Green Climate Fund supports PES initiatives as part of broader climate adaptation and mitigation efforts.

3. Strengths and Challenges

Public financing offers scalability and alignment with national policy goals, but it may face challenges such as limited budgets, bureaucratic inefficiencies, or competing political priorities. Ensuring equitable distribution of public funds and minimizing dependence on external aid are critical for long-term sustainability.

Private Financing Models

Private sector engagement in PES schemes involves businesses, NGOs, or individuals acting as buyers of ecosystem services. This model is often market-driven, with funding tied to specific outcomes such as carbon sequestration, water purification, or biodiversity offsets.

1. Corporate Investment

Businesses participate in PES schemes to meet regulatory requirements, fulfill CSR goals, or secure resources critical to their operations. For example, a beverage company might pay upstream landowners to adopt sustainable farming practices that protect water quality. Similarly, companies in high-emission sectors may purchase carbon credits generated by reforestation projects.

2. Voluntary Contributions

Private funding can also come from voluntary sources, such as donations from individuals or NGOs committed to conservation. For instance, environmental organizations might finance PES schemes to protect critical habitats or endangered species.

3. Strengths and Challenges

Private financing is flexible and innovative, with the potential to attract significant resources. However, it often focuses on ecosystem services with clear market value, leaving less tangible benefits, such as cultural services, underfunded. Additionally, profit-driven motives may conflict with broader environmental or social objectives, requiring careful alignment of priorities.

Blended Financing Models

Blended financing combines public and private resources to leverage the strengths of both sectors. These models are particularly effective for large, complex PES schemes that address multiple objectives, such as climate resilience, poverty alleviation, and ecosystem restoration.

1. Public-Private Partnerships (PPPs)

In PPPs, governments and private entities collaborate to finance and manage PES schemes. Governments often provide the regulatory framework and initial funding, while private partners contribute capital, expertise, or technology. For example, a PPP might fund mangrove restoration, with government agencies ensuring legal protection and private companies financing the planting and maintenance efforts.

2. Innovative Financial Instruments

Blended financing can also involve tools such as green bonds, environmental trust funds, or payments for carbon credits. These instruments pool resources from diverse stakeholders and channel them into PES initiatives. For instance, green bonds issued by municipal governments can fund urban NBS projects like green roofs or restored wetlands.

3. Strengths and Challenges

Blended models maximize resource availability and distribute risks among stakeholders. They are particularly effective for scaling PES schemes by attracting private investment to complement public funding. However, coordinating multiple actors and balancing competing interests can be challenging, requiring robust governance frameworks.

Comparative Insights

Each financing model has unique advantages and limitations. Public financing is ideal for delivering public goods, private financing excels in market-driven initiatives, and blended models offer scalability and resilience. The choice of model depends on the scheme's objectives, the availability of resources, and the socio-economic context. In many cases, combining approaches can address gaps and enhance overall effectiveness.

Summary

Public, private, and blended financing models are all critical to the success of PES schemes. By understanding the strengths and limitations of each approach, stakeholders can design financing strategies that align with the goals of the scheme while ensuring sustainability and scalability. Leveraging diverse funding sources is essential for integrating PES with NBS, driving long-term environmental and social benefits.

Role of Carbon Markets, Green Bonds, and Environmental Taxes

Innovative financial mechanisms such as carbon markets, green bonds, and environmental taxes play a crucial role in funding PES schemes and scaling NBS. These instruments mobilize resources, align economic incentives with environmental objectives, and create sustainable revenue streams for PES initiatives. By leveraging these tools, stakeholders can enhance the financial viability of PES schemes while addressing global environmental challenges like climate change, biodiversity loss, and ecosystem degradation.

Carbon Markets

Carbon markets are platforms where carbon credits are traded, providing a financial mechanism for reducing greenhouse gas emissions. These markets support PES schemes by monetizing the carbon sequestration benefits of NBS initiatives, such as reforestation or wetland restoration.

1. Compliance Markets

Compliance markets, such as those established under cap-and-trade systems, require companies to offset their emissions by purchasing carbon credits. For example, a reforestation project under a PES scheme might generate carbon credits by sequestering carbon, which can then be sold to companies needing to meet regulatory obligations. This creates a direct financial incentive for landowners and communities to participate in conservation activities.

2. Voluntary Carbon Markets

Voluntary markets allow companies, organizations, and individuals to purchase carbon credits to offset their emissions outside regulatory frameworks. These markets are growing as businesses commit to achieving net-zero emissions and seek cost-effective ways to offset unavoidable emissions. PES schemes tied to NBS, such as agroforestry or mangrove restoration, can benefit from these markets by supplying verified carbon credits.

3. Challenges and Opportunities

While carbon markets generate significant funding for PES schemes, challenges include ensuring the additionality and permanence of carbon sequestration and preventing leakage. Robust verification mechanisms and standardized methodologies are essential for maintaining the integrity of carbon markets.

Green Bonds

Green bonds are fixed-income financial instruments specifically designed to fund projects with environmental benefits. They provide a reliable and scalable source of funding for PES schemes and NBS initiatives.

1. Funding Large-Scale Projects

Green bonds are well-suited for financing large-scale NBS projects, such as urban green infrastructure or landscape restoration. Municipalities, governments, and corporations can issue green bonds to raise capital for initiatives like wetland restoration or afforestation programs that deliver measurable ecosystem services.

2. Attracting Private Investment

Green bonds appeal to institutional and private investors seeking environmentally sustainable investments. By offering competitive returns while supporting ecological objectives, green bonds bridge the gap between financial markets and environmental conservation.

3. Strengths and Limitations

Green bonds provide long-term funding, making them ideal for PES schemes requiring significant upfront investments. However, ensuring transparency and accountability in the use of proceeds is critical to maintaining investor confidence. Certification and reporting standards, such as those provided by the Climate Bonds Initiative, help verify the environmental impact of funded projects.

Environmental Taxes

Environmental taxes, such as carbon taxes, water abstraction fees, or pollution charges, are designed to internalize the external costs of environmental degradation. Revenues from these taxes can be directly allocated to fund PES schemes and NBS initiatives.

1. Carbon Taxes

Carbon taxes impose a price on carbon emissions, encouraging businesses and individuals to reduce their carbon footprint. Governments can channel the revenues generated by carbon taxes into PES schemes that incentivize carbon sequestration, such as forest preservation or soil carbon storage.

2. Water and Pollution Charges

Taxes on water use or pollution discharge create financial incentives for sustainable resource management. For example, a water abstraction fee can fund PES schemes that protect upstream watersheds, ensuring clean and reliable water supplies for downstream users.

3. Behavioral Incentives

Environmental taxes also drive behavioral change by making environmentally harmful practices more expensive. This aligns economic activities with conservation goals, supporting the broader integration of PES schemes with policy frameworks.

4. Strengths and Challenges

Environmental taxes are a reliable and predictable funding source for PES initiatives. However, their implementation can face resistance from businesses and consumers, requiring careful design to balance environmental objectives with economic considerations.

Integrating Financial Mechanisms with PES

The integration of carbon markets, green bonds, and environmental taxes with PES schemes offers significant potential for scaling NBS initiatives. These instruments can be used individually or in combination to address diverse financing needs:

1. Blended Financing

Blending funds from green bonds, carbon markets, and environmental taxes can enhance resource mobilization and risk-sharing, making PES schemes more resilient to market or policy fluctuations.

2. Policy Alignment

Governments can align these instruments with broader environmental policies, such as climate action plans or biodiversity strategies, to maximize their impact and ensure coherence.

3. Strengthening Local Economies

Revenues from these mechanisms can support local economies by funding community-based PES initiatives, providing income opportunities, and enhancing ecosystem services critical to livelihoods.

Summary

Carbon markets, green bonds, and environmental taxes provide essential financial tools for scaling PES schemes and supporting NBS. By monetizing ecosystem services, attracting private investment, and generating public revenues, these mechanisms bridge the gap between conservation goals and financial sustainability. Leveraging these tools effectively requires robust governance, transparent reporting, and alignment with broader environmental and social objectives, ensuring long-term benefits for ecosystems and communities alike.

International Funding Sources: Multilateral Development Banks, UN Mechanisms, and Philanthropy

International funding sources are vital for the implementation and scaling of PES schemes and NBS. These sources, which include multilateral development banks, United Nations (UN) mechanisms, and philanthropic contributions, provide financial and technical support to address global environmental challenges such as climate change, biodiversity loss, and ecosystem degradation. Their contributions enable PES schemes to operate in regions where local or national funding is insufficient, ensuring that critical ecosystem services are conserved and enhanced.

Multilateral Development Banks (MDBs)

MDBs play a crucial role in financing large-scale environmental projects, including PES schemes. Examples include the World Bank, the Asian Development Bank, and the African Development Bank. These institutions provide loans, grants, and technical assistance to governments and organizations implementing PES-linked NBS initiatives.

1. Funding Mechanisms

MDBs support PES schemes through instruments such as concessional loans, grants, and project-based financing. For instance, the World Bank's Forest Carbon Partnership Facility (FCPF) provides funding to countries for reducing emissions from deforestation and forest degradation, often using PES mechanisms.

2. Capacity-Building and Technical Support

MDBs often complement financial assistance with capacity-building programs, such as training in monitoring and evaluation or developing legal frameworks for PES schemes. This technical support strengthens institutional capacity and enhances the effectiveness of PES initiatives.

3. Regional Focus

MDBs also address region-specific challenges, such as water scarcity in the Middle East or deforestation in the Amazon. By tailoring their funding to local contexts, MDBs enable PES schemes to target critical ecosystem services in vulnerable areas.

4. Challenges and Opportunities

While MDB funding offers significant resources, accessing these funds can be complex, requiring detailed proposals and adherence to strict compliance standards. Strengthening partnerships and streamlining application processes can enhance the accessibility of MDB financing.

UN Mechanisms

The United Nations provides various funding mechanisms to support PES and NBS initiatives, particularly through programs focused on climate action, biodiversity, and sustainable development.

1. Green Climate Fund (GCF)

The GCF is a key UN mechanism supporting PES schemes as part of broader climate mitigation and adaptation strategies. For example, the GCF finances projects that use PES to incentivize reforestation or sustainable land management, contributing to carbon sequestration and resilience-building.

2. Global Environment Facility (GEF)

The GEF funds projects that align with international environmental agreements, such as the CBD. PES schemes targeting biodiversity conservation, such as habitat protection or species recovery, often receive GEF support.

3. UN-REDD Program

The United Nations Collaborative Program on Reducing Emissions from Deforestation and Forest Degradation (UN-REDD) integrates PES into its strategies to combat deforestation. Payments are made to landowners or communities for maintaining forest cover and reducing carbon emissions.

4. Challenges and Opportunities

UN funding mechanisms often require alignment with specific global objectives, which may limit flexibility. However, their ability to mobilize substantial resources and foster international collaboration makes them invaluable for scaling PES schemes.

Philanthropic Contributions

Philanthropy provides a flexible and often innovative source of funding for PES schemes. Contributions from private foundations, corporations, and high-net-worth individuals support a wide range of conservation and sustainability initiatives.

1. Private Foundations

Foundations such as the Rockefeller Foundation, the Gordon and Betty Moore Foundation, and the Bezos Earth Fund are major contributors to environmental projects. These organizations fund PES schemes that address biodiversity, climate resilience, and sustainable livelihoods.

2. Corporate Philanthropy

Many corporations contribute to PES schemes through CSR initiatives. For instance, a company may fund PES projects to offset its carbon footprint or support biodiversity conservation in its supply chain.

3. Flexibility and Innovation

Philanthropic funding often allows for greater flexibility in project design and implementation compared to public funding. For example, foundations may support pilot PES schemes, enabling experimentation and innovation before scaling successful models.

4. Challenges and Opportunities

Philanthropy, while substantial, is often unpredictable and reliant on donor priorities. Building long-term partnerships with donors and aligning PES objectives with philanthropic goals can enhance funding reliability.

Summary

Multilateral development banks, UN mechanisms, and philanthropic contributions are essential components of the international funding landscape for PES and NBS. These sources provide critical financial support, technical expertise, and global collaboration, enabling PES schemes to address environmental and social challenges at scale. By leveraging these resources effectively, stakeholders can ensure the long-term success and sustainability of PES initiatives, contributing to a healthier planet and more resilient communities.

Challenges in Mobilizing Finance and Potential Solutions

Mobilizing finance for PES schemes and NBS is critical for addressing global environmental challenges. However, securing adequate and sustainable funding is fraught with challenges, ranging from limited awareness and competing priorities to technical and institutional barriers. Addressing these challenges requires innovative strategies and collaborative efforts to unlock the financial potential of PES and NBS initiatives.

Challenges in Mobilizing Finance

1. Limited Awareness and Understanding

Many stakeholders, including policymakers, businesses, and communities, lack awareness of the value of ecosystem services and the role of PES in supporting NBS. This often results in insufficient prioritization of PES schemes in budgets or investment plans.

2. Perceived Risk and Uncertainty

Investors and funders often view PES schemes as risky due to uncertainties around ecosystem service delivery, long project timelines, and the need for robust monitoring. The absence of standardized metrics for measuring outcomes further compounds these concerns.

3. Fragmented Funding Sources

PES schemes often rely on a mix of public, private, and philanthropic funding. Fragmentation across these sources can lead to inefficiencies, duplication of efforts, and gaps in financing.

4. Lack of Institutional Capacity

In many regions, especially in developing countries, institutions lack the capacity to design, implement, and monitor PES schemes effectively. This limits their ability to attract and manage funding from diverse sources.

5. High Transaction Costs

The administrative and operational costs of setting up and maintaining PES schemes, including stakeholder engagement, contract management, and monitoring, can deter participation and reduce financial viability.

Potential Solutions

1. Raising Awareness and Building Partnerships

Public awareness campaigns, capacity-building initiatives, and multi-stakeholder dialogues can enhance understanding of the benefits of PES and NBS. Partnerships between governments, businesses, and NGOs can also foster collaboration and pool resources, increasing financial support.

2. Innovative Financial Instruments

Developing and scaling financial tools such as green bonds, carbon credits, and impact investment funds can attract new sources of capital. For example, PES schemes linked to carbon markets can monetize the sequestration benefits of NBS projects, providing a steady revenue stream.

3. Blended Financing Models

Combining public, private, and philanthropic funds through blended financing mechanisms can mitigate risks and leverage resources. Public funds can act as a catalyst, de-risking investments and encouraging private sector participation.

4. Improved Metrics and Monitoring Systems

Developing standardized metrics for measuring ecosystem services and leveraging technology such as remote sensing and AI can enhance transparency and build investor confidence. Reliable monitoring systems reduce perceived risks and demonstrate the effectiveness of PES schemes.

5. Reducing Transaction Costs

Streamlining administrative processes, using digital platforms for contract management, and adopting community-based monitoring approaches can lower transaction costs and make PES schemes more accessible and efficient.

6. Strengthening Institutional Capacity

Investing in institutional capacity-building through training, technical assistance, and knowledge-sharing platforms can empower local and national institutions to design and manage PES schemes effectively, increasing their ability to mobilize funding.

Summary

Mobilizing finance for PES and NBS requires overcoming challenges related to awareness, risk perception, institutional capacity, and fragmented funding. By raising awareness, developing innovative financing tools, and strengthening institutional frameworks, stakeholders can unlock new funding opportunities and ensure the long-term sustainability of PES initiatives. These efforts are crucial for scaling NBS, delivering environmental and social benefits, and addressing global sustainability challenges.

Chapter 5: Monitoring and Evaluating PES for NBS

Monitoring and evaluation (M&E) are essential components of PES schemes, particularly when supporting NBS. These processes ensure that PES schemes achieve their intended outcomes by tracking progress, assessing impacts, and identifying areas for improvement. Effective M&E provides accountability, enhances transparency, and builds trust among stakeholders, while also demonstrating the value of investments in PES and NBS initiatives. This chapter explores the principles, methods, and tools for M&E in the context of PES schemes, highlighting their role in measuring ecosystem service delivery, ensuring compliance, and supporting adaptive management. By addressing the challenges and opportunities in M&E, the chapter provides practical guidance for designing robust evaluation frameworks that enhance the effectiveness and scalability of PES for NBS.

Importance of M&E in PES Schemes

M&E are critical components of PES schemes, ensuring their effectiveness, accountability, and long-term sustainability. By systematically assessing the implementation and outcomes of PES initiatives, M&E provides valuable insights into their impact on ecosystem services and the stakeholders involved. This process is essential for building trust, optimizing performance, and scaling successful models.

Ensuring Ecosystem Service Delivery

The primary goal of PES schemes is to incentivize actions that enhance or maintain ecosystem services. M&E ensures that these services are being delivered as intended by tracking changes in ecological indicators. For example, a PES scheme for reforestation may monitor forest cover, biodiversity levels, and carbon sequestration over time. Reliable data from M&E helps demonstrate the scheme's effectiveness and validates the financial investments made by buyers.

Enhancing Accountability and Transparency

M&E fosters accountability among all stakeholders, including service providers, buyers, and intermediaries. By establishing clear metrics and regularly reporting outcomes, M&E ensures that all parties adhere to their commitments. This transparency builds trust and credibility, encouraging continued participation and investment. For instance, service providers are more likely to honor their obligations when they know their actions are being monitored, while buyers gain confidence that their payments are linked to measurable results.

Supporting Adaptive Management

Ecosystems are dynamic, and PES schemes often operate in complex socio-ecological contexts. M&E provides the data needed to adapt to changing conditions and improve scheme performance. By identifying challenges, inefficiencies, or unintended consequences early, stakeholders can make informed adjustments to program design, implementation, or payment structures. For example, if monitoring reveals that reforestation efforts are hindered by invasive species, targeted interventions can be implemented to address the issue.

Demonstrating Additionality and Avoiding Leakage

M&E is crucial for verifying additionality, ensuring that PES schemes deliver benefits beyond what would have occurred without intervention. Baseline assessments and ongoing monitoring allow stakeholders to measure the incremental impact of PES activities. Additionally, M&E helps detect and mitigate leakage, where environmental benefits in one area are offset by negative impacts elsewhere. For instance, monitoring land use changes can ensure that conservation efforts do not displace deforestation to adjacent areas.

Building Stakeholder Confidence

Effective M&E strengthens stakeholder confidence by providing evidence of the scheme's success. This is particularly important for securing long-term funding and attracting new participants. Clear documentation of environmental and social outcomes enhances the credibility of PES schemes and their alignment with broader sustainability goals, such as the United Nations Sustainable Development Goals (SDGs).

Challenges and Opportunities

While M&E is essential, it can be resource-intensive and technically challenging, particularly in remote or resource-constrained settings. Leveraging technology, such as remote sensing, GIS tools, and automated data collection, can enhance efficiency and reduce costs. Community-based monitoring approaches also offer opportunities for engaging local stakeholders and integrating traditional knowledge into M&E processes.

Summary

Monitoring and evaluation are indispensable for the success of PES schemes, ensuring that ecosystem services are delivered effectively, stakeholders are accountable, and adaptive management is supported. By providing transparency, validating additionality, and demonstrating outcomes, M&E enhances the credibility and scalability of PES initiatives, making them a reliable tool for financing and implementing NBS.

Key Performance Indicators for NBS Outcomes: Environmental, Social, and Economic Metrics

Key performance indicators (KPIs) are essential for evaluating the effectiveness of NBS implemented through PES schemes. These indicators help measure the environmental, social, and economic outcomes of NBS initiatives, providing a comprehensive understanding of their impacts and guiding adaptive management. By using well-defined metrics, stakeholders can assess whether NBS projects are achieving their intended objectives and align efforts with broader sustainability goals.

Environmental Metrics

Environmental KPIs focus on assessing the ecological impacts of NBS initiatives. These indicators measure changes in ecosystem health, biodiversity, and the delivery of ecosystem services.

1. **Carbon Sequestration**

• **Metric**: Tons of CO_2 equivalent (tCO_2e) sequestered annually.

• **Relevance**: Tracks the role of reforestation, afforestation, and soil carbon storage in mitigating climate change.

• **Example**: A PES-funded mangrove restoration project might monitor carbon sequestration rates using remote sensing and soil sampling.

2. **Water Quality and Quantity**

• **Metric**: Concentration of pollutants (e.g., nitrogen, phosphorus) and flow rates in water bodies.

• **Relevance**: Measures the effectiveness of NBS in improving water quality and regulating water flow through wetland restoration or watershed management.

• **Example**: A watershed protection scheme may assess reductions in sedimentation and nutrient runoff using field sampling.

3. **Biodiversity Conservation**

• **Metric**: Species richness, population trends of key species, or habitat area restored.

• **Relevance**: Tracks the impact of NBS on conserving flora and fauna, particularly in regions with high biodiversity.

• **Example**: Monitoring the return of native species in a restored forest can demonstrate the success of habitat restoration efforts.

4. Soil Health

• **Metric**: Soil organic carbon content, erosion rates, or nutrient availability.

• **Relevance**: Evaluates the impact of agroforestry or sustainable farming practices on soil productivity and resilience.

• **Example**: A PES scheme incentivizing no-till farming may track improvements in soil structure and fertility.

Social Metrics

Social KPIs measure the impact of NBS projects on human well-being, community engagement, and equity. These indicators ensure that social co-benefits are considered alongside environmental outcomes.

1. Community Engagement

• **Metric**: Number of stakeholders actively participating in NBS initiatives, such as local workshops or co-management agreements.

• **Relevance**: Measures the level of community involvement, which is crucial for the long-term success of PES schemes.

• **Example**: A community-led forest conservation project may track attendance at planning meetings and the adoption of conservation practices.

2. Equity and Inclusion

• **Metric**: Percentage of marginalized groups (e.g., women, indigenous peoples) benefiting from PES payments or capacity-building programs.

• **Relevance**: Ensures that NBS projects address social equity and include diverse stakeholders.

• **Example**: A PES scheme targeting watershed restoration might report the proportion of payments going to women-led households.

3. Access to Ecosystem Services

• **Metric**: Number of people gaining improved access to clean water, food, or natural resources due to NBS interventions.

• **Relevance**: Tracks the direct benefits of restored ecosystems on local communities.

• **Example**: Monitoring the increase in water availability for downstream users after wetland restoration.

4. Cultural and Recreational Benefits

• **Metric**: Visitor numbers to restored natural areas or satisfaction levels among community members.

• **Relevance**: Highlights the non-material benefits of NBS, such as recreation and cultural enrichment.

• **Example**: A PES-funded urban green space project might assess the frequency of recreational use and community feedback.

Economic Metrics

Economic KPIs assess the financial and livelihood impacts of NBS projects, ensuring that they contribute to local and regional economic development.

1. Income Generation

• **Metric**: Average income increase among PES recipients or new job opportunities created.

• **Relevance**: Demonstrates the economic benefits of NBS for local communities.

• **Example**: A reforestation scheme might monitor income gains from PES payments or sustainable timber production.

2. Cost-Effectiveness

• **Metric**: Cost per ton of carbon sequestered or per hectare of habitat restored.

• **Relevance**: Evaluates the financial efficiency of NBS compared to conventional solutions.

• **Example**: Comparing the costs of wetland restoration to those of building gray infrastructure for flood control.

3. Market Access

• **Metric**: Number of participants gaining access to new markets for sustainable products, such as certified timber or organic crops.

• **Relevance**: Tracks the role of NBS in enhancing economic opportunities.

• **Example**: An agroforestry project might report on the sales of shade-grown coffee or other sustainable products.

4. Ecosystem Service Valuation

• **Metric**: Economic value of ecosystem services provided, such as water filtration or climate regulation.

• **Relevance**: Quantifies the financial benefits of NBS initiatives.

• **Example**: Valuing the water purification benefits of a restored wetland to justify public and private investment.

Integrating KPIs Across Dimensions

The integration of environmental, social, and economic KPIs ensures a holistic evaluation of NBS outcomes. For instance, a PES scheme targeting mangrove restoration might measure carbon sequestration (environmental), income generation for local fishers (economic), and the inclusion of marginalized groups in decision-making (social). This multi-dimensional approach highlights the co-benefits of NBS and strengthens their case for scalability.

Summary

Key performance indicators provide the tools to measure and communicate the success of NBS initiatives supported by PES schemes. By integrating environmental, social, and economic metrics, stakeholders can assess progress, build trust, and ensure that NBS projects deliver long-term benefits. Robust KPIs enable adaptive management, ensuring that PES schemes remain effective and aligned with broader sustainability goals.

Technologies for M&E: Remote Sensing, IoT, and AI

Technologies such as remote sensing, the Internet of Things (IoT), and artificial intelligence (AI) are revolutionizing M&E processes in PES schemes and NBS. These tools enhance the precision, efficiency, and scalability of M&E, enabling stakeholders to track ecosystem service delivery, assess outcomes, and ensure compliance more effectively. By integrating these technologies, PES schemes can overcome traditional barriers like high costs and limited accessibility, ensuring better decision-making and adaptive management.

Remote Sensing

Remote sensing uses satellite imagery, drones, and aerial photography to collect data on ecosystems from a distance. It is particularly effective for monitoring large-scale or inaccessible areas, such as forests, wetlands, and agricultural landscapes.

1. Applications in PES and NBS

• **Land Use and Cover Changes**: Remote sensing can track changes in land cover, such as deforestation, reforestation, or wetland restoration, providing critical data on the progress of NBS initiatives.

• **Carbon Sequestration**: Satellite data can estimate biomass and carbon stocks, enabling accurate measurements of carbon sequestration in forest-based PES schemes.

• **Water Quality and Flow**: Remote sensing can monitor parameters like sedimentation, vegetation health, and water levels in rivers and wetlands, supporting watershed management projects.

2. Strengths

• Large-scale coverage and high temporal resolution allow for regular updates and comprehensive monitoring.

• Non-invasive and cost-effective for tracking ecosystem changes over time.

3. **Challenges**

• Requires technical expertise to analyze and interpret data.

• Limited accuracy for small-scale or highly localized changes.

4. **Example**: A PES scheme supporting mangrove restoration may use satellite imagery to monitor mangrove cover, assess biomass changes, and identify areas requiring additional intervention.

IoT

The IoT involves interconnected sensors and devices that collect and transmit real-time data. In PES and NBS contexts, IoT technologies are used to monitor ecosystem parameters, such as soil quality, water levels, and air temperature, with high spatial and temporal accuracy.

1. **Applications in PES and NBS**

• **Soil and Water Monitoring**: IoT sensors measure soil moisture, nutrient levels, and water quality, providing data essential for sustainable agriculture and watershed protection.

• **Wildlife Tracking**: GPS-enabled devices track animal movements and habitat use, supporting biodiversity conservation efforts.

• **Climate Data Collection**: Weather stations equipped with IoT devices monitor temperature, rainfall, and humidity, informing adaptive management in climate-sensitive NBS projects.

2. Strengths

• Real-time data collection enables timely decision-making and adaptive management.

• High precision and scalability for site-specific monitoring.

3. Challenges

• High initial setup costs and potential maintenance issues in remote areas.

• Requires reliable communication networks for data transmission.

4. **Example**: An agroforestry PES scheme might deploy soil sensors to monitor moisture levels, enabling farmers to optimize irrigation practices and maintain healthy tree cover.

AI

AI leverages advanced algorithms to process and analyze large datasets, providing insights that would be difficult or time-consuming to obtain manually. In PES and NBS, AI is used for pattern recognition, predictive modeling, and decision support.

1. Applications in PES and NBS

• **Data Analysis**: AI processes satellite and IoT data to identify trends, such as deforestation hotspots or carbon stock changes.

• **Predictive Modeling**: AI models forecast the impact of NBS interventions, such as flood risk reduction or biodiversity restoration, under different scenarios.

• **Automated Monitoring**: AI-powered systems analyze images from drones or camera traps to track wildlife populations or detect illegal activities, such as logging or poaching.

2. Strengths

• Handles vast and complex datasets efficiently, providing actionable insights.

• Improves accuracy and reduces human error in data interpretation.

3. Challenges

• Requires high-quality data for training algorithms, which may not always be available.

• High initial development costs and need for technical expertise.

4. **Example**: An AI model could analyze satellite data to predict the long-term carbon sequestration potential of a reforestation project, guiding payment structures in a PES scheme.

Integrating Technologies for Comprehensive M&E

While each technology has unique strengths, integrating remote sensing, IoT, and AI can create a robust M&E framework. For example, IoT sensors can collect real-time data on soil moisture, which is then analyzed by AI models to identify patterns and predict trends. Meanwhile, remote sensing can validate these insights at a landscape scale, ensuring consistency and reliability.

Opportunities and Challenges

1. Opportunities

• **Scalability**: These technologies enable the monitoring of large areas and complex ecosystems, making them ideal for scaling PES and NBS initiatives.

• **Cost Efficiency**: Over time, technological advancements reduce costs, making these tools more accessible.

2. **Challenges**

• **Data Integration**: Combining datasets from different technologies requires standardized protocols and skilled personnel.

• **Equity Concerns**: Ensuring that local communities have access to and benefit from these technologies is critical for inclusive and equitable PES schemes.

Summary

Remote sensing, IoT, and AI are transforming M&E in PES schemes and NBS initiatives, offering precise, scalable, and cost-effective solutions. By integrating these technologies, stakeholders can enhance transparency, accountability, and efficiency, ensuring the success and sustainability of ecosystem service projects. As these tools continue to evolve, they will play an increasingly vital role in addressing global environmental challenges.

Addressing Leakage, Permanence, and Additionality Concerns

Leakage, permanence, and additionality are critical concerns in the implementation of PES schemes, particularly those supporting NBS. These challenges can undermine the effectiveness and credibility of PES initiatives, making it essential to address them through robust planning, monitoring, and adaptive management. Ensuring that ecosystem service benefits are genuinely delivered, sustained over time, and additional to what would have occurred without intervention is key to the success of PES schemes.

Leakage

Leakage occurs when the environmental benefits achieved in one area are offset by negative impacts elsewhere. For example, a PES scheme promoting forest conservation in one region might displace deforestation to another, reducing the net environmental gain.

1. Types of Leakage

• **Activity Displacement**: Deforestation or resource extraction activities shift to areas outside the PES project boundary.

• **Market Leakage**: Reduced supply of ecosystem goods, such as timber, increases their market price, incentivizing exploitation elsewhere.

2. Mitigation Strategies

• **Comprehensive Planning**: Designing PES schemes at a landscape or regional scale to account for interconnected ecosystems and market dynamics.

• **Monitoring Beyond Project Boundaries**: Expanding monitoring efforts to include adjacent areas helps identify and mitigate leakage early.

• **Policy Integration**: Aligning PES schemes with broader land-use policies and enforcement mechanisms reduces the risk of activity displacement.

Permanence

Permanence refers to the long-term sustainability of the environmental benefits achieved through PES schemes. Without permanence, gains such as carbon sequestration or biodiversity conservation may be reversed, particularly when land use changes after the PES agreement ends.

1. Challenges to Permanence

• **External Pressures**: Economic development, land-use changes, or political instability may threaten long-term conservation outcomes.

• **Natural Disturbances**: Events such as wildfires, floods, or pests can negate the benefits of NBS initiatives.

2. Mitigation Strategies

• **Long-Term Contracts**: Extending the duration of PES agreements ensures ongoing protection of ecosystem services.

• **Legal and Institutional Safeguards**: Establishing conservation easements or protected area designations helps secure the permanence of outcomes.

• **Adaptive Management**: Regular monitoring and flexible management plans allow for adjustments in response to changing conditions.

• **Insurance Mechanisms**: Financial tools, such as carbon buffers or risk-sharing funds, provide compensation for losses due to unforeseen events.

Additionality

Additionality ensures that the benefits delivered by PES schemes are above and beyond what would have occurred without the intervention. For example, paying for reforestation in an area where forests were already regenerating naturally would fail to meet the additionality criterion.

1. Challenges to Additionality

• **Baseline Uncertainty**: Difficulty in determining what would have happened in the absence of the PES scheme.

• **Overlapping Incentives**: Existing policies, subsidies, or conservation efforts may already incentivize the desired outcomes.

2. Mitigation Strategies

• **Accurate Baseline Assessments**: Conducting detailed studies to establish clear baselines against which progress can be measured.

• **Robust Monitoring**: Tracking the implementation of agreed-upon actions ensures that payments are tied to genuine improvements.

• **Exclusion of Pre-Existing Actions**: Ensuring that PES payments are only made for activities initiated because of the scheme.

Summary

Addressing leakage, permanence, and additionality is critical to the success and credibility of PES schemes. By adopting comprehensive planning, robust monitoring, and adaptive management practices, stakeholders can mitigate these challenges and ensure that the environmental, social, and economic benefits of PES and NBS are genuine, lasting, and scalable. These efforts are essential for maximizing the impact of PES schemes and building confidence among funders and participants.

Chapter 6: Scaling Up PES to Accelerate NBS Implementation

Scaling up PES is essential to maximize the potential of NBS in addressing global environmental challenges such as climate change, biodiversity loss, and ecosystem degradation. While PES schemes have demonstrated success at local and regional levels, expanding their scope and impact requires overcoming financial, institutional, and technical barriers. This chapter explores strategies for scaling up PES initiatives, including innovative financing mechanisms, policy integration, stakeholder engagement, and the use of emerging technologies. By addressing these opportunities and challenges, the chapter provides a roadmap for expanding PES schemes to accelerate the implementation and mainstreaming of NBS on a global scale.

Pathways to Scaling PES Schemes: From Pilots to Large-Scale Initiatives

Scaling PES schemes from small-scale pilot projects to large-scale initiatives is critical for maximizing their impact on ecosystem conservation and NBS. Successful scaling requires addressing challenges, building on lessons from pilot projects, and implementing strategies that expand PES initiatives while maintaining their effectiveness, inclusivity, and sustainability.

Lessons from Pilot Projects

Pilot projects provide valuable insights into the design, implementation, and management of PES schemes. These small-scale initiatives test approaches, identify challenges, and build stakeholder capacity before broader rollouts.

1. Testing Feasibility

Pilots allow stakeholders to assess whether PES schemes are suitable for specific contexts. For example, a watershed protection scheme may test whether upstream communities are willing and able to adopt conservation practices in exchange for payments from downstream users.

2. Building Stakeholder Trust

By demonstrating tangible benefits, pilots build trust among stakeholders, including service providers, buyers, and intermediaries. Successful pilots often encourage broader participation and support for scaling.

3. Identifying Challenges

Pilots help identify barriers such as unclear property rights, insufficient monitoring capacity, or logistical constraints. Addressing these issues during the pilot phase ensures smoother transitions to larger-scale initiatives.

4. Refining Metrics and Processes

Pilot projects enable the refinement of M&E frameworks, payment structures, and governance mechanisms. These refinements are crucial for scaling effectively.

Enhancing Financial Sustainability

Scaling PES schemes requires sustainable and diversified funding sources. Transitioning from donor-dependent pilots to financially self-sufficient programs is a key step in scaling.

1. Blended Finance Models

Combining public funding, private investment, and philanthropic contributions can provide the resources needed for large-scale initiatives. For example, governments can de-risk private investments by providing guarantees or seed funding.

2. Innovative Financial Instruments

Tools like green bonds, carbon credits, and environmental taxes can mobilize additional resources for PES schemes. For instance, a reforestation initiative might generate revenue through carbon markets, supporting both pilot and large-scale phases.

3. Payment Mechanisms

Adopting scalable payment mechanisms, such as digital platforms, reduces transaction costs and enhances accessibility for service providers, especially in remote areas.

Policy and Institutional Integration

Scaling PES schemes requires alignment with broader policy frameworks and the establishment of robust institutional support systems.

1. Policy Alignment

Integrating PES schemes into national or regional policies, such as climate action plans or biodiversity strategies, provides the legal and regulatory foundation for scaling. For instance, including PES in NDCs under the Paris Agreement can secure international funding and political commitment.

2. Institutional Strengthening

Capacity-building for local and national institutions ensures effective governance, monitoring, and enforcement at scale. Partnerships with multilateral organizations, NGOs, and private sector actors can enhance institutional capacity.

3. Cross-Sectoral Collaboration

Engaging multiple sectors, such as agriculture, forestry, and urban planning, ensures that PES schemes address interconnected challenges. For example, a landscape-level PES initiative might involve agricultural practices, forest conservation, and water management.

Leveraging Technology

Technology plays a crucial role in scaling PES schemes by improving efficiency, transparency, and monitoring capabilities.

1. Remote Sensing and GIS

Satellite imagery and geographic information systems (GIS) enable large-scale monitoring of land use changes, carbon sequestration, and ecosystem health, reducing the cost and complexity of M&E.

2. Digital Platforms

Online platforms facilitate payment processing, data collection, and stakeholder engagement, streamlining operations and increasing participation.

3. AI

AI-driven analytics enhance decision-making by identifying patterns, predicting outcomes, and optimizing resource allocation in large-scale PES schemes.

Engaging Stakeholders

Broad stakeholder engagement ensures that scaled-up PES schemes are inclusive, equitable, and supported by all participants.

1. Community Participation

Engaging local communities in design and implementation fosters ownership and ensures that benefits reach those most dependent on ecosystem services. Capacity-building initiatives, such as training and technical support, empower communities to participate effectively.

2. Private Sector Involvement

Scaling requires increased participation from the private sector, particularly in financing and technical expertise. Businesses can act as buyers of ecosystem services, contributing to sustainable supply chains and corporate social responsibility goals.

3. Public Awareness

Raising awareness about the benefits of PES schemes among policymakers, investors, and the general public builds support for scaling efforts.

Overcoming Challenges

Scaling PES schemes presents unique challenges, but strategic planning and adaptive management can address these issues.

1. Equity and Inclusion

Ensuring that scaled initiatives benefit marginalized communities and small-scale service providers is critical for social sustainability.

Transparent benefit-sharing mechanisms and participatory governance structures can address equity concerns.

2. Avoiding Leakage and Ensuring Permanence

Large-scale PES schemes must implement robust monitoring to prevent leakage and ensure the permanence of ecosystem services. For instance, integrating regional or landscape-level approaches minimizes the risk of displaced activities undermining project goals.

3. Maintaining Additionality

Demonstrating that scaled initiatives deliver benefits beyond what would have occurred without intervention is essential for maintaining credibility and securing funding.

Scaling Through Regional and Global Networks

Collaborating with regional and global networks accelerates scaling by sharing knowledge, resources, and best practices.

1. Regional Collaborations

Transboundary initiatives, such as watershed management across countries, leverage shared resources and address ecosystem challenges at scale.

2. Global Platforms

International organizations, such as the UN, Green Climate Fund, and Global Environment Facility, provide funding, technical assistance, and platforms for scaling PES schemes worldwide.

Summary

Scaling PES schemes from pilot projects to large-scale initiatives is essential for addressing global environmental challenges and maximizing the potential of NBS. By building on pilot successes, leveraging financial and technological resources, and fostering inclusive stakeholder engagement, PES schemes can be expanded to deliver sustainable and impactful ecosystem services at a broader scale. Strategic planning and adaptive management will ensure that these initiatives achieve their intended environmental, social, and economic benefits.

Role of Partnerships: Public-Private Collaboration and Community Involvement

Partnerships are critical for the success and scalability of PES schemes and NBS. Effective collaboration among public institutions, private entities, and communities ensures that these initiatives are inclusive, sustainable, and impactful. By leveraging the unique strengths of each partner, these alliances enhance resource mobilization, governance, and local engagement, addressing complex socio-ecological challenges. This section explores the roles of public-private collaboration and community involvement in designing, implementing, and scaling PES schemes.

Public-Private Collaboration

Public-private partnerships (PPPs) combine the regulatory authority of governments with the innovation, efficiency, and financial resources of private entities. These collaborations are instrumental in bridging funding gaps, improving governance, and scaling PES initiatives.

1. Leveraging Financial Resources

• **Role of Public Institutions**: Governments often provide seed funding, regulatory frameworks, and tax incentives to encourage private sector investment in PES schemes. For example, public funding can de-risk private investments in NBS by covering initial implementation costs.

• **Role of Private Entities**: Businesses contribute through direct payments for ecosystem services, investments in green infrastructure, or CSR initiatives. For instance, a beverage company might fund watershed protection projects to secure clean water for its operations.

2. Innovative Solutions

• The private sector brings expertise in technology, market-based solutions, and supply chain management to PES schemes. For example, companies may develop digital platforms for payment processing or monitoring systems that enhance transparency and efficiency.

• Public institutions provide oversight and alignment with policy objectives, ensuring that private initiatives support broader sustainability goals.

3. Examples of Collaboration

• A PPP for mangrove restoration may involve government agencies providing legal protection for coastal areas, while private companies finance planting efforts and develop eco-tourism opportunities.

• In urban settings, public funding might support the creation of green roofs, with private developers contributing through mandatory green building certifications.

4. Challenges and Solutions

• **Challenges**: Misaligned priorities between public and private partners can lead to inefficiencies or conflicts. Additionally, ensuring transparency and accountability in financial flows is critical for maintaining trust.

• **Solutions**: Establishing clear roles, responsibilities, and benefit-sharing mechanisms in partnership agreements fosters collaboration. Regular communication and stakeholder consultations help address conflicting interests.

Community Involvement

Engaging local communities is essential for the long-term success and equity of PES schemes. Communities are often the primary stewards of ecosystems, and their participation ensures that conservation efforts are context-specific, culturally appropriate, and sustainable.

1. Local Knowledge and Stewardship

• Communities possess valuable traditional knowledge about ecosystems, including sustainable land-use practices, biodiversity, and climate resilience. Incorporating this knowledge into PES schemes enhances the effectiveness of interventions.

• Community members often serve as on-the-ground stewards, implementing conservation activities such as reforestation, soil restoration, or sustainable agriculture.

2. Benefit Sharing

• Equitable benefit-sharing mechanisms ensure that communities receive fair compensation for their contributions to ecosystem services. Payments can take the form of direct financial incentives, capacity-building programs, or community infrastructure improvements.

• Transparent agreements that outline payment structures and performance metrics build trust and encourage active participation.

3. Capacity Building

• Providing training, technical assistance, and access to resources empowers communities to participate effectively in PES schemes. For example, farmers may receive training in agroforestry techniques or financial literacy to manage PES payments.

• Strengthening local governance structures, such as cooperatives or community forest user groups, ensures collective decision-making and equitable benefit distribution.

4. Examples of Community Involvement

• A PES scheme for watershed management may engage upstream communities in planting native vegetation, with payments linked to improvements in downstream water quality.

• In biodiversity conservation projects, indigenous groups may monitor wildlife populations or patrol protected areas, receiving compensation for their efforts.

5. Challenges and Solutions

• **Challenges**: Power imbalances, lack of capacity, and unclear land tenure can limit community participation. Additionally, external pressures, such as economic development or land-use changes, may undermine conservation efforts.

• **Solutions**: Addressing land tenure issues, fostering inclusive governance, and integrating PES schemes into broader development plans can mitigate these challenges. Building long-term partnerships with communities enhances trust and resilience.

Synergies Between Public-Private and Community Partnerships

Integrating public-private collaboration with community involvement creates a holistic approach to PES schemes. Governments and private entities can provide funding, technical expertise, and policy support, while communities contribute local knowledge, labor, and stewardship.

1. Examples of Synergy

• In a forest conservation initiative, governments may enforce legal protections, private companies finance monitoring technologies, and communities implement reforestation activities.

• Coastal resilience projects may involve public funding for mangrove restoration, corporate support for eco-tourism development, and local participation in maintenance and monitoring.

2. Shared Benefits

• Collaborative approaches ensure that all stakeholders share the benefits of PES schemes, including enhanced ecosystem services, improved livelihoods, and strengthened environmental governance.

• By fostering inclusivity and accountability, these partnerships build trust and long-term support for conservation efforts.

Summary

Partnerships are at the heart of effective PES schemes, combining the strengths of public institutions, private entities, and local communities. Public-private collaboration provides the financial and technical resources needed to scale initiatives, while community involvement ensures their sustainability and equity. By fostering synergies among stakeholders, PES schemes can achieve their full potential, delivering environmental, social, and economic benefits on a larger scale.

Building Financial Sustainability in Scaled PES Initiatives

Financial sustainability is a cornerstone of scaling PES initiatives. As PES schemes expand, ensuring reliable, long-term funding becomes increasingly important to maintain operations, deliver ecosystem services, and foster stakeholder trust. A sustainable financial framework involves diversified funding sources, cost-efficiency, and mechanisms to adapt to evolving economic and environmental conditions.

Diversifying Funding Sources

Relying on a single funding source increases the risk of financial instability. Scaled PES initiatives benefit from a mix of public, private, and philanthropic funding.

1. Public Funding

Governments can provide baseline financing through environmental taxes, subsidies, or budget allocations. For example, carbon taxes or water abstraction fees can be channeled into PES schemes, ensuring steady support for ecosystem service providers.

2. Private Sector Engagement

The private sector contributes significantly through CSR initiatives, voluntary offsets, or direct payments for ecosystem services. For instance, businesses reliant on clean water may invest in watershed protection projects.

3. Blended Finance

Combining public, private, and philanthropic funds reduces financial risk and attracts investment. Public funding can act as a catalyst, de-risking private sector contributions or covering upfront costs.

4. Innovative Financial Instruments

Tools like green bonds, carbon credits, and payments for biodiversity offsets generate additional revenue streams. For example, a PES scheme involving reforestation might sell carbon credits to offset emissions.

Enhancing Cost Efficiency

Cost-efficient operations are essential for maintaining financial sustainability, especially as PES initiatives scale.

1. Streamlining Administrative Processes

Digital platforms for contract management, payment distribution, and monitoring reduce administrative overheads. Automation minimizes human error and accelerates processes.

2. Community-Based Monitoring

Engaging local communities in monitoring and enforcement reduces costs while building stakeholder ownership. For example, community members can track forest cover or water quality using low-cost tools and mobile applications.

3. Economies of Scale

Scaling PES schemes often reduces per-unit costs, such as transaction fees or monitoring expenses. Larger initiatives can negotiate better terms with service providers or leverage shared infrastructure.

Ensuring Long-Term Revenue

Building mechanisms for continuous revenue generation is vital for sustaining PES schemes over time.

1. Endowment Funds and Trusts

Establishing dedicated funds or trusts ensures ongoing financial support. Interest generated from these funds can cover operational costs and provide stability during economic downturns.

2. Market Integration

Linking PES schemes to established markets, such as carbon trading or sustainable agriculture, creates consistent demand for ecosystem services. Certification schemes, such as organic or fair-trade labels, also enhance market value.

3. Adaptive Financial Models

Flexible payment structures that adjust to changing economic conditions, such as inflation or currency fluctuations, ensure that participants remain adequately incentivized.

Building Stakeholder Confidence

Financial sustainability is closely tied to stakeholder trust and participation.

1. Transparent Financial Management

Regular reporting on financial flows, outcomes, and returns builds confidence among funders and participants. Audits and third-party evaluations enhance credibility.

2. Equitable Benefit Sharing

Ensuring that payments reach marginalized communities and small-scale providers fosters inclusivity and local support, essential for long-term success.

Summary

Building financial sustainability in scaled PES initiatives requires a multi-pronged approach that includes diversified funding, cost-efficient operations, and mechanisms for continuous revenue generation. By fostering stakeholder trust and leveraging innovative financial tools, PES schemes can achieve long-term viability while delivering significant environmental, social, and economic benefits. Financial sustainability ensures that PES initiatives remain impactful and resilient, supporting NBS at scale.

Overcoming Barriers to Scaling: Capacity-Building, Regulatory Reforms, and Technological Innovation

Scaling PES initiatives to achieve significant environmental and social impacts requires addressing key barriers. These include insufficient institutional and technical capacity, fragmented regulatory frameworks, and limited access to technology. Overcoming these challenges involves strategic capacity-building, targeted regulatory reforms, and the integration of technological innovations. Together, these approaches enable PES schemes to expand while maintaining their effectiveness and inclusivity.

Capacity-Building

Strengthening the capacity of stakeholders—governments, communities, and private sector actors—is essential for scaling PES initiatives.

1. Institutional Strengthening

- **Challenges**: Many regions lack the institutional frameworks to manage large-scale PES schemes effectively, including mechanisms for monitoring, enforcement, and benefit distribution.

- **Solutions**: Investments in training, knowledge-sharing platforms, and human resources help build the necessary expertise. For instance, workshops on contract management and ecosystem service valuation empower institutions to handle scaled initiatives.

2. Community Empowerment

- **Challenges**: Local communities often lack the technical skills and financial literacy needed to participate fully in PES schemes.

- **Solutions**: Capacity-building programs provide training in sustainable practices, monitoring techniques, and financial management. Supporting the establishment of community-based organizations ensures collective decision-making and equitable participation.

3. Private Sector Engagement

- **Challenges**: Businesses may lack awareness of the opportunities and benefits of participating in PES schemes.

- **Solutions**: Outreach programs, incentives, and partnerships demonstrate the value of PES initiatives to corporate sustainability goals, increasing private sector involvement.

Regulatory Reforms

Fragmented or inadequate regulatory frameworks often hinder the scaling of PES schemes. Reforming policies to align with the goals of PES and NBS is critical for overcoming these barriers.

1. Clarifying Land Tenure and Rights

• **Challenges**: Unclear or disputed land tenure undermines the credibility and inclusivity of PES schemes, particularly in marginalized communities.

• **Solutions**: Legal reforms that recognize customary land rights and secure tenure provide the foundation for equitable participation and long-term sustainability.

2. Integrating PES into National Policies

• **Challenges**: PES schemes are often treated as standalone projects, limiting their impact and scalability.

• **Solutions**: Incorporating PES into national strategies, such as climate action plans or biodiversity policies, ensures alignment with broader development goals and secures government support.

3. Harmonizing Cross-Sectoral Policies

• **Challenges**: Conflicting regulations in sectors like agriculture, forestry, and water management can create obstacles.

• **Solutions**: Regulatory coherence across sectors fosters synergy and enhances the scalability of PES schemes.

Technological Innovation

Technology plays a transformative role in scaling PES schemes by enhancing efficiency, transparency, and monitoring capabilities.

1. M&E

• **Challenges**: Scaling M&E is resource-intensive, particularly in remote or large areas.

• **Solutions**: Remote sensing, IoT devices, and AI-powered analytics improve data collection and analysis, making large-scale monitoring feasible and cost-effective.

2. Digital Platforms

• **Challenges**: High transaction costs can deter participation, particularly for small-scale providers.

• **Solutions**: Digital platforms streamline contract management, payment processing, and data sharing, reducing administrative burdens and improving accessibility.

3. Knowledge Sharing

• **Challenges**: Limited access to best practices and case studies constrains replication and scaling.

• **Solutions**: Online platforms and tools facilitate knowledge exchange, enabling stakeholders to learn from successful PES initiatives worldwide.

Summary

Overcoming barriers to scaling PES schemes requires a multifaceted approach combining capacity-building, regulatory reforms, and technological innovation. By strengthening institutions, aligning policies, and leveraging technology, stakeholders can address key challenges and unlock the full potential of PES initiatives. These efforts ensure that scaled PES schemes deliver meaningful and lasting benefits, supporting NBS on a global scale.

Chapter 7: Social and Ethical Dimensions of PES and NBS

The success and sustainability of PES schemes and NBS depend on addressing their social and ethical dimensions. These initiatives often operate in diverse socio-economic and cultural contexts, where equity, inclusivity, and community well-being are critical considerations. This chapter explores the social and ethical implications of PES and NBS, including the challenges of equitable benefit-sharing, the inclusion of marginalized groups, and the potential for unintended social consequences. By highlighting these dimensions, the chapter provides strategies for ensuring that PES and NBS initiatives are not only environmentally effective but also socially just and ethically sound.

Ensuring Equity and Inclusivity: Participation of Marginalized Communities

Equity and inclusivity are critical to the success and sustainability of PES schemes and NBS. Marginalized communities, including indigenous peoples, women, and small-scale landowners, often have a significant stake in ecosystem services due to their reliance on natural resources for livelihoods. Ensuring their meaningful participation in PES schemes not only promotes social justice but also enhances the effectiveness of conservation efforts by leveraging local knowledge and fostering community ownership. This section examines strategies to ensure equity and inclusivity in PES initiatives, focusing on addressing barriers, promoting participation, and ensuring fair benefit-sharing.

Barriers to Participation

Marginalized communities face unique challenges that limit their ability to participate in and benefit from PES schemes.

1. Lack of Land Tenure Security

• **Challenge**: Unclear or insecure land tenure often prevents marginalized groups from accessing PES opportunities. Without formal recognition of their land rights, these communities may be excluded from payments or face the risk of displacement.

• **Solution**: Legal reforms to recognize customary land rights and secure tenure for marginalized communities provide the foundation for equitable participation in PES schemes.

2. Limited Awareness and Capacity

• **Challenge**: Marginalized groups often lack awareness of PES opportunities or the technical capacity to meet the requirements of participation, such as monitoring or reporting ecosystem services.

• **Solution**: Targeted outreach and capacity-building programs can bridge this gap. Workshops, training sessions, and simplified application processes empower communities to engage effectively.

3. Power Imbalances

• **Challenge**: Unequal power dynamics between stakeholders can result in marginalized groups having limited influence over decision-making or benefit-sharing arrangements.

• **Solution**: Inclusive governance structures, such as community-based organizations or multi-stakeholder platforms, ensure that marginalized voices are heard and respected.

Strategies for Promoting Participation

1. Engaging Indigenous Peoples

• **Importance**: Indigenous peoples often possess deep knowledge of ecosystems and play a crucial role in conservation. However, they are frequently excluded from PES initiatives.

• **Approach**: Co-design PES schemes with indigenous communities, integrating traditional knowledge into conservation practices and ensuring that cultural values are respected. For example, involving indigenous groups in forest management programs can enhance biodiversity outcomes and foster trust.

2. Empowering Women

• **Importance**: Women, especially in rural areas, are often primary users and managers of natural resources but face systemic barriers to participation in PES schemes.

• **Approach**: Promote gender equity by ensuring women have equal access to training, resources, and decision-making opportunities. Gender-sensitive approaches, such as providing childcare support during workshops or targeting women-led initiatives, can enhance their involvement.

3. Supporting Small-Scale Landowners

• **Importance**: Small-scale landowners are key stakeholders in many ecosystems but may lack the resources to adopt sustainable practices required for PES participation.

• **Approach**: Offer financial incentives, technical support, and flexible contracts tailored to the needs of small-scale landowners. Reducing transaction costs and simplifying participation criteria can make PES schemes more accessible.

Ensuring Fair Benefit-Sharing

Equity in benefit-sharing is central to ensuring that marginalized groups receive a fair share of the rewards from PES schemes.

1. Transparent Payment Structures

• **Challenge**: Complex or opaque payment systems can disadvantage marginalized participants.

• **Solution**: Develop clear and transparent payment structures that specify the basis for compensation, timelines, and conditions. Payments should reflect the opportunity costs and contributions of participants, ensuring fairness.

2. Community-Level Benefits

• **Challenge**: Individual payments may not address broader community needs or foster collective ownership.

• **Solution**: Complement individual payments with investments in community infrastructure, such as schools, healthcare, or water systems. These shared benefits enhance community support and long-term sustainability.

3. Monitoring Equity Outcomes

• **Challenge**: Without monitoring, it is difficult to ensure that benefits are distributed equitably.

• **Solution**: Include equity indicators in monitoring and evaluation frameworks, tracking the participation and benefits received by marginalized groups. Regular feedback mechanisms allow for adjustments to address inequities.

Building Inclusive Governance

1. Participatory Decision-Making

• **Importance**: Ensuring that marginalized communities have a voice in decision-making strengthens governance and fosters ownership.

• **Approach**: Establish governance structures that include representatives from marginalized groups in planning, implementation, and evaluation processes.

2. Conflict Resolution Mechanisms

• **Importance**: Disputes over land, payments, or resource use can disproportionately affect marginalized groups.

• **Approach**: Develop accessible and culturally appropriate mechanisms for resolving conflicts, ensuring that marginalized participants can seek redress without fear of retaliation.

3. Strengthening Partnerships

• **Importance**: Collaboration with NGOs, civil society organizations, and advocacy groups can amplify the voices of marginalized communities and provide additional resources for their participation.

• **Approach**: Foster partnerships that support capacity-building, knowledge exchange, and advocacy for marginalized groups.

Summary

Ensuring equity and inclusivity in PES schemes requires proactive measures to address barriers, promote participation, and share benefits fairly. By engaging marginalized communities, recognizing their rights and contributions, and fostering inclusive governance, PES initiatives can deliver not only environmental outcomes but also significant social and economic benefits. Inclusive PES schemes are more likely to succeed in the long term, as they build trust, foster local ownership, and contribute to sustainable development goals.

Land Tenure and Property Rights in PES-Linked NBS

Land tenure and property rights are critical factors in the success of PES schemes linked to NBS. These rights define who has legal or customary control over land and its resources, directly influencing participation, benefit-sharing, and long-term sustainability. Secure and well-defined land tenure systems are fundamental for PES schemes to operate effectively, as they ensure that service providers can claim payments and engage in conservation activities without fear of displacement or conflict.

Importance of Land Tenure in PES

1. Eligibility and Participation

• PES schemes often require clear evidence of land ownership or control to identify eligible participants. Unclear or insecure tenure can exclude smallholders, indigenous peoples, and other marginalized groups from participating in PES programs.

• Secure land tenure provides the foundation for long-term commitments to conservation practices, such as reforestation, agroforestry, or wetland restoration.

2. Incentivizing Sustainable Land Use

• When land tenure is secure, landowners and users are more likely to invest in sustainable practices. For instance, farmers with clear rights are more inclined to adopt soil conservation techniques or protect forest cover under a PES scheme.

3. Avoiding Conflicts

• Clear property rights reduce disputes over land use and ownership, fostering trust among stakeholders. This is especially important in areas where overlapping claims or historical grievances may otherwise hinder PES implementation.

Challenges Related to Land Tenure in PES

1. Informal or Customary Land Tenure

• In many regions, especially in developing countries, land is governed by informal or customary systems that lack legal recognition. This can create challenges in verifying eligibility and enforcing PES agreements.

• Marginalized groups, such as indigenous peoples or nomadic communities, are particularly vulnerable, as their customary rights may not be acknowledged by formal legal systems.

2. Overlapping Claims

• In areas with multiple stakeholders, such as communal lands or shared forests, disputes over ownership or usage rights can arise. These conflicts can delay or derail PES implementation.

3. Land Tenure Insecurity

• Without secure tenure, participants may be hesitant to engage in long-term conservation practices for fear of losing access to their land. In some cases, external pressures, such as land grabs or development projects, can undermine PES initiatives.

4. Transaction Costs

• Clarifying land tenure and resolving disputes often involve significant costs, including legal fees, surveys, and administrative processes. These costs can be prohibitive, particularly for small-scale PES initiatives.

Strategies to Address Land Tenure Challenges

1. **Legal Recognition of Customary Rights**

• Governments and policymakers can promote inclusivity by recognizing customary land tenure systems. For example, legal frameworks can formalize the rights of indigenous and local communities, ensuring their eligibility for PES schemes.

• Participatory land mapping and registration processes can document and protect customary claims, reducing disputes.

2. **Conflict Resolution Mechanisms**

• Establishing accessible and transparent mechanisms for resolving land disputes is essential for ensuring smooth implementation of PES schemes. These mechanisms should involve impartial mediators and respect the rights of all stakeholders.

3. **Collective Land Management**

• In areas with shared or communal land, collective management agreements can provide a framework for equitable participation. For example, community forest user groups can enter into PES agreements collectively, with payments distributed based on agreed-upon rules.

4. **Capacity-Building and Legal Support**

• Providing legal assistance and capacity-building programs can empower marginalized groups to assert their land rights. Workshops on land tenure laws, negotiation skills, and dispute resolution enhance community participation in PES schemes.

Examples of Land Tenure's Role in NBS

1. Reforestation and Agroforestry

• In reforestation PES schemes, secure tenure ensures that participants have the legal authority to plant and manage trees over the long term. This is critical for generating benefits like carbon sequestration and biodiversity conservation.

2. Watershed Management

• PES programs that rely on upstream landowners to implement sustainable practices require clear ownership or usage rights. For instance, payments for reducing agricultural runoff depend on the landowner's ability to make and enforce decisions about land use.

3. Indigenous-Led Conservation

• Indigenous communities with recognized land rights have successfully participated in PES schemes focused on protecting biodiversity or reducing deforestation. Recognizing these rights strengthens the role of indigenous peoples as stewards of critical ecosystems.

Summary

Land tenure and property rights are pivotal for the success of PES-linked NBS initiatives. Secure and equitable tenure systems enable broad participation, promote sustainable land use, and minimize conflicts. Addressing tenure challenges through legal recognition, conflict resolution, and capacity-building ensures that PES schemes are inclusive and effective. By fostering trust and stability, clear land rights contribute to the long-term sustainability and scalability of PES and NBS efforts.

Ethical Considerations: Commodification of Ecosystem Services

The commodification of ecosystem services, central to the operation of PES schemes, raises important ethical considerations. By assigning monetary value to ecosystem services such as carbon sequestration, water purification, and biodiversity conservation, PES schemes create market-based incentives for environmental stewardship. However, this approach is not without controversy. Critics argue that commodification risks oversimplifying complex ecological and cultural values, privileging certain stakeholders over others, and potentially undermining intrinsic environmental ethics. This section explores the ethical implications of commodifying ecosystem services and offers strategies to address these concerns.

The Concept of Commodification

Commodification involves framing ecosystem services as economic goods that can be bought, sold, or traded. While this market-based approach is designed to incentivize conservation and sustainable practices, it inherently simplifies the multifaceted value of ecosystems.

1. Benefits of Commodification

• **Economic Incentives**: By attaching monetary value to ecosystem services, PES schemes encourage individuals, communities, and corporations to invest in conservation.

• **Operational Efficiency**: Commodification enables standardized payment structures and measurable outcomes, making PES schemes more scalable and transparent.

• **Mainstreaming Conservation**: Integrating ecosystem services into economic systems raises awareness of their importance and generates funding for their protection.

2. Risks of Commodification

• **Reductionism**: By focusing solely on economic value, commodification may ignore the ecological, cultural, and spiritual significance of ecosystems.

• **Market Dependency**: Commodification ties conservation efforts to market dynamics, which can fluctuate based on economic conditions, potentially destabilizing PES initiatives.

Ethical Concerns

1. Equity and Access

• **Concern**: Commodification risks privileging stakeholders with financial resources, such as corporations or wealthy landowners, over marginalized communities. This can exacerbate inequalities in access to ecosystem services and decision-making power.

• **Example**: A carbon offset project may prioritize payments to large-scale landowners, sidelining smallholders or indigenous groups who depend on the same ecosystems.

2. Intrinsic Value of Nature

• **Concern**: Ecosystems and biodiversity are often valued for their intrinsic worth, independent of human utility. Commodification risks undermining this perspective by reducing nature to a commodity.

• **Example**: Framing a forest solely in terms of its carbon sequestration potential ignores its cultural, spiritual, and aesthetic significance to local communities.

3. Ethical Trade-Offs

• **Concern**: Decisions about which ecosystem services to commodify involve trade-offs that may prioritize certain services (e.g., carbon sequestration) over others (e.g., cultural heritage). This can lead to unintended ecological and social consequences.

• **Example**: A PES scheme focusing on carbon offsets might incentivize monoculture plantations, which could harm biodiversity and local livelihoods.

4. Commodification and Environmental Ethics

• **Concern**: Market-based approaches risk fostering a transactional view of conservation, where environmental protection becomes contingent on financial incentives rather than moral or ethical imperatives.

Addressing Ethical Concerns

1. Incorporating Non-Monetary Values

• **Approach**: PES schemes can integrate non-monetary values by recognizing the cultural, spiritual, and ecological significance of ecosystems. For example, community-led conservation initiatives may emphasize traditional ecological knowledge alongside financial incentives.

2. Ensuring Equity and Inclusion

• **Approach**: Equitable benefit-sharing mechanisms ensure that marginalized communities receive fair compensation and have a voice in decision-making processes. This fosters inclusivity and reduces inequalities.

• **Example**: Co-designing PES schemes with indigenous groups ensures that their cultural and spiritual values are respected and integrated into the project.

3. Balancing Trade-Offs

• **Approach**: Decision-makers should adopt a holistic perspective, assessing the broader ecological and social impacts of PES schemes. Multi-criteria analysis tools can help balance competing priorities, such as biodiversity, carbon storage, and cultural heritage.

4. Strengthening Ethical Governance

• **Approach**: Establishing transparent and participatory governance frameworks ensures accountability and ethical oversight. Independent advisory boards or community-based monitoring systems can safeguard ethical principles in PES operations.

5. Promoting Environmental Stewardship

• **Approach**: PES schemes can complement market-based incentives with educational campaigns that emphasize intrinsic environmental values. This dual approach reinforces the ethical imperative for conservation.

Navigating the Ethical Balance

Balancing the practical benefits of commodification with ethical considerations requires careful design and adaptive management. While commodification can drive much-needed investment in conservation, PES schemes must account for the full spectrum of ecosystem values and prioritize fairness, inclusion, and long-term sustainability.

Summary

The commodification of ecosystem services presents both opportunities and challenges for PES-linked NBS initiatives. By assigning monetary value to ecosystem services, commodification creates powerful incentives for conservation. However, addressing the ethical concerns associated with reductionism, inequity, and trade-offs is critical to ensuring that PES schemes are socially just and environmentally sound. Integrating non-monetary values, promoting inclusivity, and fostering ethical governance will help strike a balance between economic efficiency and moral responsibility, enabling PES initiatives to deliver meaningful and equitable outcomes.

Building Trust and Resolving Stakeholder Conflicts

Trust and conflict resolution are central to the success of PES schemes and NBS. These initiatives involve diverse stakeholders, including landowners, communities, private sector actors, and government agencies, whose interests and priorities may not always align. Building trust and addressing conflicts proactively ensures cooperation, equitable outcomes, and long-term sustainability. This section explores strategies to foster trust and resolve conflicts among stakeholders in PES-linked NBS initiatives.

Importance of Trust in PES Schemes

Trust is a cornerstone of successful collaboration in PES initiatives. It enables stakeholders to work together effectively, honor commitments, and engage in meaningful dialogue.

1. Transparency

• **Challenge**: Lack of transparency in decision-making, financial flows, or monitoring can lead to mistrust among participants.

• **Solution**: Providing open access to information about payment structures, project goals, and evaluation metrics fosters accountability and reduces suspicion. For instance, regular public reporting and stakeholder meetings ensure that all parties are informed and engaged.

2. Consistency

• **Challenge**: Inconsistent policies or enforcement can undermine trust, particularly among marginalized groups.

• **Solution**: Establishing clear, consistent rules and applying them fairly across all stakeholders builds confidence in the scheme.

3. Inclusivity

• **Challenge**: Excluding certain stakeholders from decision-making processes can lead to feelings of disenfranchisement and resistance.

• **Solution**: Ensuring that all relevant groups, including indigenous peoples, women, and small-scale landowners, have a voice in governance strengthens trust and ownership.

Sources of Conflict in PES Schemes

Conflicts in PES initiatives often arise from competing interests, resource allocation, or differing perceptions of fairness.

1. Resource Use Conflicts

• **Example**: Landowners may face restrictions on resource use due to conservation agreements, while local communities may depend on those resources for livelihoods.

• **Resolution**: Participatory planning processes that balance conservation goals with community needs reduce tensions. For instance, integrating sustainable use practices into PES agreements can benefit both ecosystems and local livelihoods.

2. Benefit-Sharing Disputes

• **Example**: Disagreements may occur over how payments are distributed, particularly in communal or shared land scenarios.

• **Resolution**: Transparent and equitable benefit-sharing mechanisms, combined with clear contractual agreements, minimize disputes.

3. Cultural and Ethical Differences

• **Example**: Commodification of ecosystem services may conflict with traditional or spiritual values held by indigenous communities.

• **Resolution**: Respecting and integrating cultural values into PES design, such as recognizing traditional knowledge and practices, builds trust and reduces conflict.

Strategies for Building Trust

1. Effective Communication

• Regular, open communication between stakeholders fosters understanding and reduces misunderstandings. Facilitating dialogue through workshops, community meetings, or digital platforms ensures that concerns are addressed in a timely manner.

2. Participatory Decision-Making

• Involving stakeholders in every stage of the PES process—from design to implementation—builds trust and ensures that diverse perspectives are considered. Participatory approaches also promote a sense of ownership and accountability.

3. Third-Party Facilitation

• Independent mediators or advisory boards can play a neutral role in managing conflicts, building trust, and ensuring fairness. For example, a third-party organization might oversee benefit-sharing arrangements or facilitate negotiations.

4. Capacity-Building

• Providing training and technical support empowers stakeholders, particularly marginalized groups, to participate effectively. Capacity-building initiatives demonstrate a commitment to inclusivity, reinforcing trust.

Conflict Resolution Mechanisms

1. Grievance Redress Systems

• Establishing accessible and transparent grievance mechanisms ensures that stakeholders can voice concerns and seek resolution without fear of retaliation. These systems should be culturally appropriate and tailored to local contexts.

2. Collaborative Problem-Solving

• Engaging stakeholders in collaborative approaches, such as joint fact-finding or co-design of solutions, reduces adversarial dynamics and fosters mutual understanding. For example, landowners and communities might work together to develop sustainable land-use plans.

3. Formal Agreements

• Clear, enforceable contracts reduce ambiguity and prevent disputes. Agreements should outline roles, responsibilities, payment structures, and conflict resolution processes.

4. Continuous Monitoring and Feedback

• Regularly assessing project outcomes and soliciting stakeholder feedback helps identify and address potential conflicts early. Adaptive management ensures that PES schemes remain responsive to evolving needs and challenges.

Examples of Successful Conflict Resolution

1. Watershed Management

• In a PES initiative involving upstream landowners and downstream water users, regular consultations and a joint decision-making committee helped resolve conflicts over water use, fostering long-term cooperation.

2. Forest Conservation

• In a communal forest PES scheme, disputes over benefit distribution were mitigated by establishing a community trust fund managed by an independent board. This approach ensured transparency and equitable allocation of resources.

Summary

Building trust and resolving conflicts are essential for the success and scalability of PES schemes linked to NBS. By fostering transparency, inclusivity, and collaboration, stakeholders can overcome disputes and work toward shared goals. Implementing effective communication strategies, robust grievance mechanisms, and participatory governance structures ensures that PES initiatives are both equitable and sustainable, delivering lasting benefits for ecosystems and communities.

Chapter 8: Future Directions for PES and NBS Integration

As global challenges such as climate change, biodiversity loss, and resource degradation intensify, integrating PES schemes with NBS offers a promising pathway for sustainable development. This chapter explores emerging trends, opportunities, and challenges in advancing the integration of PES and NBS. It highlights the potential for innovative financing mechanisms, policy alignments, and technological advancements to enhance the scalability and effectiveness of these initiatives. Additionally, the chapter examines the role of global collaboration and inclusive governance in shaping the future of PES and NBS, emphasizing the need for adaptive strategies to address evolving environmental and social priorities.

Emerging Trends: Digital Platforms, Blockchain for Transparency, and Ecosystem Credit Markets

The integration of digital technologies into PES schemes and NBS is transforming how these initiatives are designed, implemented, and scaled. Emerging trends such as digital platforms, blockchain technology, and ecosystem credit markets are addressing key challenges in transparency, efficiency, and scalability. These innovations provide stakeholders with tools to enhance trust, reduce costs, and unlock new financing opportunities, making PES schemes more effective and accessible.

Digital Platforms for PES

Digital platforms are revolutionizing the administration of PES schemes by streamlining processes such as stakeholder engagement, payment distribution, and monitoring.

1. Simplifying Transactions

• **Challenge**: Traditional PES schemes often face high transaction costs and administrative inefficiencies, which can deter participation.

• **Solution**: Digital platforms provide centralized systems for managing contracts, tracking payments, and recording ecosystem service delivery. For example, mobile applications enable small-scale landowners to submit proof of compliance and receive payments efficiently.

2. Enhancing Accessibility

• **Challenge**: Marginalized communities and smallholders often struggle to access PES schemes due to geographic or technological barriers.

• **Solution**: Digital platforms can bridge this gap by offering multilingual interfaces, user-friendly designs, and offline functionalities. These tools ensure broader participation, even in remote areas with limited connectivity.

3. Data Collection and Reporting

• **Challenge**: Monitoring ecosystem services over large areas is resource-intensive and prone to delays.

• **Solution**: Digital platforms integrate with IoT devices, remote sensing tools, and GIS technologies to collect and analyze real-time data. For instance, sensors tracking water quality or forest cover can automatically update dashboards accessible to all stakeholders.

4. Examples

• Platforms like Connect4Climate and Plan Vivo facilitate the design and management of PES projects while fostering collaboration among participants.

Blockchain for Transparency

Blockchain technology provides a decentralized and immutable ledger, ensuring transparency and accountability in PES schemes. This innovation addresses longstanding challenges in financial management and trust among stakeholders.

1. Enhancing Trust Through Immutable Records

• **Challenge**: Stakeholders often question the fairness and reliability of financial flows and project outcomes in PES schemes.

• **Solution**: Blockchain creates transparent records of transactions, payments, and project milestones. For example, each payment from buyers to service providers can be recorded and verified on a blockchain ledger, ensuring that funds reach intended recipients.

2. Smart Contracts for Automation

• **Challenge**: Delays in payment processing and disputes over terms can hinder PES operations.

• **Solution**: Smart contracts, programmed on blockchain platforms, automatically execute payments once predefined conditions are met. For instance, a carbon sequestration project might trigger payments to landowners only after verified increases in biomass are recorded.

3. Reducing Fraud and Corruption

• **Challenge**: Fraudulent claims and corruption undermine the credibility of PES schemes, particularly in regions with weak governance.

• **Solution**: Blockchain's decentralized nature prevents data manipulation and ensures that only verified information is recorded, minimizing opportunities for fraud.

4. Examples

• Initiatives such as CarbonChain and Verra are exploring blockchain-based solutions to enhance transparency in carbon offset markets and PES-linked projects.

Ecosystem Credit Markets

Ecosystem credit markets are emerging as a vital mechanism for monetizing ecosystem services and scaling PES initiatives. These markets provide a platform for trading credits linked to services such as carbon sequestration, water purification, and biodiversity conservation.

1. Carbon Credits

• **Relevance**: Carbon markets remain the most established form of ecosystem credit trading, with PES schemes generating credits through activities like reforestation, agroforestry, and wetland restoration.

• **Example**: Landowners participating in a PES scheme may sell verified carbon credits on compliance or voluntary markets, creating a sustainable revenue stream.

2. Water Quality Trading

• **Relevance**: PES schemes can generate credits for improving water quality, such as reducing agricultural runoff or restoring riparian zones.

• **Example**: A watershed PES project may allow upstream farmers to sell water quality credits to downstream utilities or industries.

3. Biodiversity Offsets

• **Relevance**: Biodiversity credits compensate for environmental impacts caused by development projects, incentivizing investments in conservation.

• **Example**: Developers purchasing biodiversity credits might support PES initiatives that protect critical habitats or restore degraded ecosystems.

4. Market Challenges and Innovations

• **Challenges**: Ecosystem credit markets often face issues such as inconsistent standards, limited buyer awareness, and high verification costs.

• **Solutions**: Integrating blockchain technology and digital platforms improves traceability and reduces transaction costs, while certification standards, such as those developed by Gold Standard or Verra, enhance credibility.

Synergies Among Technologies

1. Interoperability

• Digital platforms can integrate blockchain for secure transaction recording and smart contracts, while also connecting with ecosystem credit markets to streamline trading.

• Example: A PES scheme using blockchain to manage payments could integrate with a digital platform to monitor ecosystem services and automatically issue credits.

2. Global Collaboration

• These technologies facilitate cross-border collaboration by standardizing processes and enhancing trust among international stakeholders, making PES schemes more scalable and attractive to investors.

Summary

Emerging trends such as digital platforms, blockchain technology, and ecosystem credit markets are transforming PES schemes and their integration with NBS. By addressing key challenges in transparency, efficiency, and scalability, these innovations unlock new opportunities for stakeholders and enhance the impact of PES initiatives. As these tools continue to evolve, they will play a critical role in shaping the future of PES and NBS, enabling stakeholders to tackle global environmental challenges more effectively.

Innovative Applications: Urban Resilience, Climate Adaptation, and Biodiversity Corridors

Innovative applications of PES schemes and NBS are unlocking new possibilities to address urban resilience, climate adaptation, and biodiversity conservation. By tailoring PES to support these areas, stakeholders can create solutions that deliver multiple benefits, including environmental restoration, social well-being, and economic sustainability. This section explores how PES schemes are being applied in urban environments, climate adaptation strategies, and the creation of biodiversity corridors.

Urban Resilience

As cities face increasing challenges from climate change, urbanization, and environmental degradation, PES schemes offer a mechanism to enhance urban resilience by incentivizing investments in green infrastructure and sustainable practices.

1. Green Infrastructure Development

• **Application**: PES schemes can support the establishment and maintenance of urban green spaces, such as parks, green roofs, and tree-lined streets, which provide ecosystem services like temperature regulation, air quality improvement, and stormwater management.

• **Example**: A city government might offer payments to property owners who install green roofs or maintain urban forests, reducing the urban heat island effect and mitigating flood risks.

2. Stormwater Management

• **Application**: Urban PES schemes can fund the implementation of permeable surfaces, wetlands, and rain gardens to manage stormwater runoff.

• **Example**: A municipality could compensate developers or homeowners for incorporating rainwater harvesting systems that reduce pressure on urban drainage systems.

3. Community Engagement

• **Application**: Engaging local communities in urban resilience efforts, such as maintaining green spaces or planting trees, ensures sustained benefits while fostering social inclusion.

• **Example**: PES programs can pay community groups to care for urban wetlands, improving biodiversity while providing recreational spaces for residents.

Climate Adaptation

PES schemes are increasingly being integrated into strategies to enhance climate adaptation, providing incentives for actions that reduce vulnerability to climate impacts and increase ecosystem resilience.

1. Coastal Protection

• **Application**: PES schemes can fund the restoration and conservation of coastal ecosystems, such as mangroves, seagrasses, and coral reefs, which act as natural barriers against storm surges and erosion.

• **Example**: A government could compensate coastal communities for protecting mangroves, which provide both carbon sequestration and storm protection benefits.

2. Water Security

• **Application**: PES initiatives can incentivize upstream communities to adopt sustainable land-use practices that protect water resources, ensuring reliable supplies for downstream users during droughts.

• **Example**: A water utility might fund PES schemes that pay farmers to reduce water-intensive crops or implement soil conservation techniques.

3. Agroforestry for Resilience

• **Application**: Agroforestry practices, supported by PES, enhance soil fertility, prevent erosion, and diversify incomes, making rural areas more resilient to climate variability.

• **Example**: Payments to smallholders for integrating trees with crops or livestock help mitigate the impacts of changing rainfall patterns while promoting biodiversity.

Biodiversity Corridors

Biodiversity corridors, which connect fragmented habitats to facilitate wildlife movement and ecological processes, are critical for conserving species and maintaining ecosystem health. PES schemes provide a financial mechanism to support the creation and maintenance of these corridors.

1. Habitat Restoration

• **Application**: PES schemes can fund reforestation, wetland restoration, and native vegetation planting in areas critical to connecting habitats.

• **Example**: Payments to landowners for restoring degraded lands adjacent to protected areas create corridors that allow species migration and genetic exchange.

2. Community-Managed Corridors

• **Application**: Engaging local communities in managing biodiversity corridors ensures their long-term success. PES can provide financial incentives for sustainable land use and conservation activities.

• **Example**: Indigenous communities might receive payments for maintaining forest corridors that connect protected areas, supporting both biodiversity and traditional livelihoods.

3. Corporate Involvement

• **Application**: Corporations can fund biodiversity corridors as part of their sustainability or biodiversity offset programs, creating partnerships with local stakeholders.

• **Example**: A mining company might support a PES scheme that funds the creation of corridors to offset habitat loss caused by its operations.

Synergies and Co-Benefits

1. Integrated Solutions

• **Synergy**: PES schemes often deliver multiple benefits simultaneously. For example, a mangrove restoration project supported by PES can enhance coastal protection, sequester carbon, and provide habitat for marine species.

• **Co-Benefit**: These integrated approaches reduce costs and maximize impact, making PES a versatile tool for addressing complex environmental challenges.

2. Collaboration Across Sectors

• **Synergy**: Urban resilience, climate adaptation, and biodiversity corridors often require coordination among governments, private entities, and communities. PES schemes provide a framework for shared investments and responsibilities.

• **Co-Benefit**: Collaborative efforts build trust and foster innovative solutions, ensuring long-term sustainability.

Challenges and Opportunities

1. Challenges

• Limited awareness and funding can constrain the implementation of PES schemes in these innovative applications.

• Ensuring equity and inclusivity in benefit-sharing remains a critical issue, particularly in urban and rural contexts.

2. **Opportunities**

• Advances in technology, such as remote sensing and digital platforms, enhance monitoring and reduce costs, making PES schemes more accessible.

• Increasing global commitments to climate action and biodiversity conservation create a favorable environment for scaling these initiatives.

Summary

Innovative applications of PES schemes in urban resilience, climate adaptation, and biodiversity corridors demonstrate their versatility and potential to address diverse environmental challenges. By providing financial incentives for sustainable practices, PES schemes enable stakeholders to create integrated solutions that deliver long-term ecological, social, and economic benefits. These applications highlight the evolving role of PES as a critical tool for building a sustainable and resilient future.

Policy Recommendations for Enhancing PES-NBS Integration

Integrating PES schemes with NBS is crucial for addressing global environmental challenges such as climate change, biodiversity loss, and resource degradation. Effective policy frameworks can enable this integration by fostering collaboration, providing financial support, and ensuring equitable outcomes. This section presents key policy recommendations to enhance the alignment of PES and NBS initiatives, emphasizing the importance of coordination, innovation, and inclusivity.

Aligning PES and NBS with National and Global Policies

1. Incorporate PES-NBS in National Strategies

• **Recommendation**: Governments should integrate PES schemes into national policies, such as climate action plans, biodiversity strategies, and sustainable development goals (SDGs).

• **Rationale**: Aligning PES with broader policy frameworks ensures consistency, fosters stakeholder buy-in, and attracts international funding. For example, including PES-NBS in NDCs under the Paris Agreement can secure climate finance and political support.

2. Strengthen International Collaboration

• **Recommendation**: Promote transboundary partnerships to address ecosystem challenges that span multiple jurisdictions, such as watershed management or biodiversity corridors.

• **Rationale**: Collaborative approaches enhance the scalability and effectiveness of PES-NBS initiatives while fostering knowledge-sharing and resource pooling.

Enhancing Financial Mechanisms

1. Develop Blended Finance Models

• **Recommendation**: Combine public, private, and philanthropic funding to de-risk investments in PES-NBS integration.

• **Rationale**: Blended finance can mobilize resources from diverse sources, ensuring the long-term sustainability of PES schemes. For instance, public funds can act as seed capital to attract private sector investment.

2. Innovate Financial Instruments

• **Recommendation**: Introduce tools such as green bonds, ecosystem credit markets, and carbon offset schemes to support PES-NBS projects.

• **Rationale**: Innovative financial instruments generate sustainable revenue streams, making it easier to scale PES initiatives. For example, carbon credits from reforestation projects can be sold to companies seeking to meet net-zero targets.

Building Institutional Capacity

1. Strengthen Governance Frameworks

• **Recommendation**: Establish clear legal and institutional frameworks to support PES-NBS integration, including property rights, monitoring mechanisms, and enforcement protocols.

• **Rationale**: Robust governance ensures accountability, reduces conflicts, and fosters stakeholder trust. Clear property rights, in particular, enable fair and transparent benefit-sharing.

2. Invest in Capacity-Building

• **Recommendation**: Provide training and technical assistance to local governments, NGOs, and communities involved in PES schemes.

• **Rationale**: Capacity-building enhances the ability of stakeholders to design, implement, and monitor PES-NBS initiatives effectively. For example, training programs on ecosystem service valuation can improve project design and decision-making.

Promoting Equity and Inclusivity

1. Ensure Fair Benefit-Sharing

• **Recommendation**: Develop policies that promote equitable distribution of benefits, particularly for marginalized groups such as indigenous peoples and small-scale landowners.

• **Rationale**: Inclusive PES schemes foster social justice and community buy-in, ensuring long-term sustainability. Transparent payment systems and participatory governance structures are critical for achieving this goal.

2. Incorporate Traditional Knowledge

• **Recommendation**: Recognize and integrate traditional ecological knowledge into PES-NBS initiatives.

• **Rationale**: Leveraging local expertise enhances the cultural relevance and effectiveness of conservation efforts. Policies that support co-management approaches strengthen the role of communities as ecosystem stewards.

Leveraging Technology and Innovation

1. Adopt Advanced Monitoring Tools

• **Recommendation**: Use technologies such as remote sensing, IoT devices, and blockchain to monitor ecosystem service delivery and ensure transparency.

• **Rationale**: Technological innovations improve efficiency, reduce costs, and enhance accountability in PES schemes. For instance, blockchain can create immutable records of payments and outcomes, fostering trust among stakeholders.

2. Support Research and Development

• **Recommendation**: Invest in research to identify best practices, optimize PES-NBS integration, and address emerging challenges.

• **Rationale**: Evidence-based policies are essential for designing effective PES schemes that deliver long-term environmental and social benefits.

Summary

Enhancing PES-NBS integration requires coordinated efforts across policy, finance, governance, and technology. By aligning PES with national and global strategies, fostering innovation, and promoting equity, policymakers can create enabling conditions for scalable and impactful initiatives. These recommendations provide a roadmap for unlocking the full potential of PES and NBS in addressing pressing environmental and socio-economic challenges.

Vision for a Global PES Framework for NBS

A global framework for PES integrated with NBS presents a transformative opportunity to address interconnected environmental challenges such as climate change, biodiversity loss, and resource degradation. By standardizing practices, fostering international collaboration, and leveraging innovative financing mechanisms, a unified global framework can scale up the effectiveness and reach of PES schemes while ensuring equitable outcomes across regions and stakeholders.

The Need for a Global Framework

1. **Addressing Fragmentation**

• **Challenge**: Current PES initiatives operate in fragmented silos, with varying standards, methodologies, and levels of success.

• **Vision**: A global framework would harmonize these efforts, creating consistent guidelines for design, implementation, and monitoring. This standardization would ensure comparability and interoperability among PES schemes, fostering trust and participation.

2. Leveraging Global Resources

• **Challenge**: Addressing large-scale environmental issues requires mobilizing significant financial and technical resources beyond the reach of individual nations or organizations.

• **Vision**: A global framework could pool resources from multilateral development banks, private investors, and philanthropic organizations, ensuring that funds are allocated efficiently and equitably to support NBS initiatives worldwide.

Key Components of a Global Framework

1. Standardized Methodologies

• **Goal**: Establish universal metrics and methodologies for measuring ecosystem services, such as carbon sequestration, biodiversity conservation, and water purification.

• **Benefit**: Consistent measurement and reporting enhance transparency and accountability, making PES schemes more attractive to funders and stakeholders.

2. Inclusive Governance Structures

• **Goal**: Create governance mechanisms that involve diverse stakeholders, including governments, private sector actors, indigenous peoples, and civil society organizations.

• **Benefit**: Inclusive decision-making ensures that the framework addresses the needs of all participants and incorporates local knowledge and values.

3. Innovative Financing Mechanisms

• **Goal**: Integrate tools like ecosystem credit markets, green bonds, and blockchain technology into the global framework.

• **Benefit**: These mechanisms provide scalable and sustainable funding options, making PES schemes more resilient to economic fluctuations.

4. Capacity-Building and Knowledge Sharing

• **Goal**: Develop global platforms for training, technical assistance, and the exchange of best practices.

• **Benefit**: Strengthening institutional and community capacity ensures that PES schemes are effectively implemented and adapted to local contexts.

Pathways to Implementation

1. Leveraging International Agreements

• **Example**: Align the global PES framework with existing multilateral agreements, such as the Paris Agreement, Convention on Biological Diversity, and the Sustainable Development Goals (SDGs).

• **Outcome**: This alignment would enhance coherence and attract funding from international climate and biodiversity initiatives.

2. Fostering Regional Cooperation

• **Example**: Establish regional hubs to coordinate PES efforts across shared ecosystems, such as transboundary rivers or forests.

• **Outcome**: Regional collaboration would address localized challenges while contributing to the broader global framework.

Vision for the Future

A global PES framework for NBS envisions a world where ecosystem services are valued and protected as critical components of sustainable development. By fostering collaboration, standardization, and innovation, such a framework would scale the impact of PES initiatives, ensuring that environmental, social, and economic benefits reach communities worldwide. This vision emphasizes equity, resilience, and sustainability, creating a pathway for addressing the planet's most pressing challenges in a unified and impactful way.

Summary

A global PES framework for NBS represents a bold step toward aligning local and regional efforts with global goals. By standardizing practices, mobilizing resources, and promoting inclusive governance, this vision ensures that PES initiatives achieve their full potential in addressing environmental and social challenges. It offers a roadmap for collaborative action, building a sustainable future where ecosystems and human well-being thrive in harmony.

Conclusion: Advancing PES for a Sustainable Future

As the global community grapples with escalating environmental challenges, PES offers a transformative approach to financing and scaling NBS. By aligning economic incentives with ecological stewardship, PES schemes bridge the gap between conservation goals and sustainable development. This concluding chapter reflects on the opportunities and challenges discussed throughout the book and highlights the critical steps needed to advance PES as a cornerstone of sustainable environmental management. From fostering equity and innovation to building robust governance and global collaboration, the path forward requires a collective commitment to unlocking the full potential of PES for a resilient and thriving planet.

Recap of PES as a Tool for Financing and Scaling NBS

PES has emerged as a powerful tool for financing and scaling NBS, addressing critical environmental challenges such as climate change, biodiversity loss, and ecosystem degradation. By incentivizing actions that conserve, restore, or sustainably manage natural ecosystems, PES schemes provide a market-based mechanism to align economic interests with ecological goals.

At its core, PES operates by assigning monetary value to ecosystem services, such as carbon sequestration, water purification, and biodiversity conservation. This approach bridges the gap between stakeholders who benefit from these services and those who provide or maintain them. By offering financial rewards to service providers, PES fosters behavioral changes and long-term commitments to conservation practices.

PES schemes also play a critical role in scaling NBS by mobilizing diverse funding sources, including public investments, private sector contributions, and philanthropic support. Innovative financial instruments, such as carbon credits and green bonds, further enhance the capacity of PES to attract and sustain funding for large-scale NBS initiatives.

Moreover, PES facilitates the integration of NBS into broader environmental and development strategies, creating synergies with global sustainability goals. Its flexibility allows it to address diverse contexts, from urban resilience projects to rural agroforestry systems and transboundary biodiversity corridors.

However, the success of PES depends on addressing challenges such as equity, governance, and monitoring. Transparent benefit-sharing mechanisms, robust legal frameworks, and inclusive decision-making processes are essential to ensure that PES schemes are socially just and environmentally effective.

In summary, PES is a dynamic and versatile tool that drives the implementation and expansion of NBS, providing critical pathways for sustainable development and global environmental resilience. By aligning financial incentives with ecosystem stewardship, PES holds significant promise for advancing a sustainable future.

Key Takeaways and Actionable Insights

PES offers a strategic pathway for financing and scaling NBS, addressing pressing global challenges such as climate change, biodiversity loss, and resource degradation. Key takeaways from this discussion emphasize the potential of PES to drive sustainable development while highlighting actionable insights for its effective implementation.

1. Economic Incentives Drive Conservation

PES schemes align financial rewards with ecological stewardship, incentivizing individuals and communities to adopt sustainable practices. By attaching monetary value to ecosystem services, PES bridges economic and environmental goals, fostering long-term commitments to conservation.

2. Integration with Policy and Global Goals

PES can amplify its impact by aligning with national and international frameworks, such as the Paris Agreement and Sustainable Development Goals (SDGs). Policymakers should incorporate PES into climate action plans, biodiversity strategies, and land-use policies to mainstream these initiatives at scale.

3. Equity and Inclusivity Are Essential

Ensuring fair benefit-sharing and active participation of marginalized groups, including smallholders and indigenous communities, is critical for the social sustainability of PES schemes. Transparent governance, capacity-building, and recognition of traditional knowledge are actionable steps to promote inclusivity.

4. Innovative Financing and Technology Enhance Impact

Tools like green bonds, ecosystem credit markets, and blockchain technology reduce costs, improve transparency, and attract diverse funding sources. Investing in advanced monitoring systems and digital platforms enhances the scalability and efficiency of PES initiatives.

5. Collaboration Strengthens Outcomes

Multi-stakeholder partnerships among governments, private sector actors, NGOs, and local communities ensure shared ownership and sustained success. Building trust through participatory approaches and clear communication is key to effective collaboration.

By embracing these insights, stakeholders can unlock the full potential of PES, leveraging it as a transformative tool to achieve environmental sustainability and resilience. With strategic action, PES can deliver lasting benefits for ecosystems, economies, and societies.

Role of Stakeholders in Driving the PES-NBS Agenda

The successful implementation and scaling of PES schemes in support of NBS require active involvement and collaboration among diverse stakeholders. Each stakeholder group plays a critical role in driving the PES-NBS agenda, contributing unique expertise, resources, and perspectives.

1. Governments

Governments provide the regulatory frameworks, policies, and funding mechanisms necessary to enable PES initiatives. By aligning PES with national strategies such as climate action plans and biodiversity goals, they create an enabling environment for NBS integration.

2. Private Sector

Businesses contribute through corporate social responsibility initiatives, direct payments for ecosystem services, and investments in green infrastructure. Their involvement brings innovation, funding, and market-based solutions, making PES initiatives financially sustainable.

3. Local Communities and Indigenous Peoples

These groups are often the primary stewards of ecosystems, contributing valuable traditional knowledge and on-the-ground conservation efforts. Their active participation ensures that PES schemes are context-specific, equitable, and sustainable.

4. Non-Governmental Organizations (NGOs)

NGOs facilitate stakeholder engagement, provide technical expertise, and advocate for equitable benefit-sharing. They play a bridging role, linking funders, communities, and policymakers.

5. Academia and Research Institutions

Researchers support PES-NBS integration by developing tools for ecosystem service valuation, monitoring outcomes, and generating evidence to inform policy and practice.

By fostering collaboration among these stakeholders, PES initiatives can deliver meaningful and lasting environmental, social, and economic benefits.

Final Reflections on the Transformative Potential of PES

PES represents a transformative approach to addressing some of the world's most pressing environmental challenges, including climate change, biodiversity loss, and ecosystem degradation. By assigning value to ecosystem services, PES bridges the gap between conservation goals and economic incentives, making sustainable practices viable and appealing to a wide range of stakeholders.

The flexibility of PES allows it to be adapted to diverse contexts, from urban resilience projects to rural reforestation efforts, creating solutions that deliver environmental, social, and economic co-benefits. Its ability to mobilize resources from public, private, and philanthropic sources ensures a steady flow of funding for NBS, even as global challenges evolve.

However, the transformative potential of PES goes beyond financing. It fosters collaboration among governments, businesses, communities, and civil society, emphasizing the shared responsibility for ecosystem stewardship. When designed with equity, transparency, and inclusivity in mind, PES schemes empower marginalized groups, integrate traditional knowledge, and enhance social cohesion.

As the world seeks sustainable pathways to resilience and prosperity, PES stands out as a dynamic and scalable tool. By prioritizing innovation, inclusivity, and accountability, PES has the potential to redefine conservation practices, driving a sustainable future for both people and the planet.

www.ingramcontent.com/pod-product-compliance
Lightning Source LLC
Chambersburg PA
CBHW071557200326

41519CB00021BB/6786